Poetry Reader for Russian Learners

Poetry Reader for Russian Learners

Edited by Julia Titus
Yale University

Illustrations by Mario Moore and Wayde McIntosh

Yale University Press
New Haven and London

Yale University Press books may be purchased in quantity for educational, business, or promotional use. For information, please e-mail sales.press@yale.edu (U.S. office) or sales@yaleup.co.uk (U.K. office).

Drawings of Pushkin, Tyutchev, Blok, Gumilev, Mayakovsky, and Yesenin are by Wayde McIntosh.
Drawings of Lermontov, Baratynsky, Fet, Annensky, Tsvetaeva, and Akhmatova are by Mario Moore.

Printed in the United States of America.

ISBN: 978-0-300-18463-1
Library of Congress Control Number: 2014952942

A catalogue record for this book is available from the British Library.

This paper meets the requirements of ANSI/NISO Z39.48-1992 (Permanence of Paper).

10 9 8 7 6 5 4 3

Contents

Acknowledgments

I would like to express my deep gratitude to Frank Miller, Lina Steiner, and Michael Pesenson for their thoughtful comments and insightful suggestions during the preparation of the manuscript. I also wish to thank Nelleke Van Deusen-Scholl and Suzanne Young at the Center for Language Study at Yale University for their encouragement and unwavering support of my work. I extend my special thanks to two outstanding artists, Wayde McIntosh and Mario Moore, for their beautiful drawings that greatly enhanced the book. I am most grateful to Vadim Staklo, Sarah Miller, and Ash Lago at YUP for their guidance during the work on the manuscript, and to my copy editor, Bojana Ristich, and my production editor, Ann-Marie Imbornoni, whose dedication, talent and diligence were invaluable in the editing process. I owe a debt of gratitude to Kirill Miniaev who created a unique companion website for the book.

Introduction

One of the many wonderful rewards of learning a foreign language is the ability to read literary masterpieces in the original. It is especially true for poetry, which was once defined as something that is not translatable. Russia is well known for its rich literary legacy, but while many great novels, such as those by Tolstoy and Dostoevsky, can be read and appreciated in translation, poetry loses much in translation. The purpose of this book is to introduce students of Russian to the great treasures of Russian poetry in the original, starting with Alexander Pushkin and the poets of the period that is known as the Golden Age of Russian poetry in the nineteenth century and moving chronologically into the twentieth century, ending with the poets of what has come to be known as the Silver Age.

All the poets selected for this anthology represent the classical canon of Russian poetry, well familiar to any Russian and taught in Russian schools as part of the school curriculum. The chosen poems reflect the essential poetic heritage of each poet, and I have aimed to include a wide variety of texts suitable for learners at different levels of language proficiency. The poems selected for each author are coded by difficulty of comprehension as follows: level (*): accessible to beginners in the first year; level (**): better suited to intermediate students; and level (***): for advanced students. The coding by level of difficulty is an approximation; it is certainly possible to read a more complex poem earlier in one's studies; it would just take more time and effort on the part of the student.

There is a brief biographical sketch for each poet, allowing the student to situate the poet within the Russian literary tradition. Each poem is accompanied by additional background information where appropriate. It is also accompanied by a glossary in the margins; a series of assignments focusing the student's attention on grammar and new lexical items, stressing root recognition and morphology in order to facilitate vocabulary retention; and general questions in English for discussion. The anthology has a companion website, and complete audio files for each poem are available for downloading through iTunes.

The audio component of the anthology is especially valuable. Learning poems by heart has been shown to have many benefits for improving foreign language skills since by listening to a poem over and over and repeating it, a student is automatically learning the correct pronunciation, new vocabulary, and correct structure. For these reasons it is highly recommended that students of all levels try to memorize the poems as they read them. In my institution many foreign language departments organize annual spring poetry readings where students recite poems and win prizes for best performance.

While the anthology is designed as an introduction to Russian poetry as it developed through the centuries and the poets and poems are listed chronologically, the poems can be read out of order if the instructor wishes to focus on a particular author or theme. Each poem contains a complete set of glosses so that it is not dependent on a previous reading. In the questions for discussion in English there are frequent calls for comparison between poems dealing with the same subject by different authors (for example, compare "Портрет" by Lermontov and "Я вас любил…" by

Pushkin or compare the winter landscape in Pushkin with that in Tyutchev), thus drawing the student's attention to the interconnectedness of the Russian literary tradition.

The anthology can be used by any learner of Russian, be he/she a currently registered student or an independent learner who has studied Russian and wishes to refresh his/her language skills. It can be a component of a language or literature course, or it can be used in a Russian for Heritage Learners class. In my courses, in addition to asking students to memorize some of the poems, I assign them presentations on an author of choice so that they can do additional research and take a more active role in their learning process. This works especially well in the Heritage Learners' courses, where students are more accustomed to memorizing poetry and want to share the poetic heritage of their parents and grandparents.

This book grew out of my firm conviction that reading poetry in the original is extremely rewarding and motivating for any student of a foreign language. It is especially true for Russian, where poetry has always been an integral part of the literary tradition and culture. I hope to inspire all readers to continue their study of Russian and share my pleasure of reading and love of poetry by providing a step-by-step guided introduction to the masterpieces of Russian poetry.

A Note on Russian Pronunciation

In learning a foreign language, it is very beneficial to learn poems by heart. Moreover, one can fully appreciate a poem only by reading it out loud since its musicality and rhythm are among its unique and inalienable elements, greatly contributing to its beauty. Most poems selected for the anthology have a very regular meter and rhyme pattern, and these will aid students greatly in memorizing the poems and learning the correct stresses. When the student practices reading the poems aloud, it will be helpful to remember a few rules of Russian pronunciation.

Unlike English—where longer words have a main stress and an auxiliary stress, typically falling on the first and third syllables—Russian has only one stress per word. For instance, note the English pronunciation of the following words: constitution, democratic, propaganda, panorama. Compare these with their Russian equivalents, which have only one stress: конститу́ция, демократи́ческий, пропага́нда, панора́ма. Consequently, one has to be careful not to automatically insert an auxillary stress into four-syllable Russian words like интере́сно, бесконе́чный, бессерде́чно, дорога́я, переме́ны, and начина́ет.

Two very important features of Russian pronunciation are vowel reduction and consonant assimilation. Vowel reduction occurs whenever a vowel is not accented. For example, compare how /a/ is pronounced in Анна. The accent falls on first vowel, so that vowel is pronounced in full strength: /á/. The second vowel is unstressed, so it undergoes vowel reduction, and the vowel is reduced to a shorter sound, /ə/, pronounced like the **a** in English **about**, **among**, and **across**.

At the beginning of a word or in the syllable before a stress, **a** and **o** are pronounced as a short /a/: Москвá /maskvá/, моя́ /mayá/, остано́вит /astanóvit/, моро́з /marós/. The **a** and **o** are pronounced /ə/ in all other unstressed syllables: остановить /astənavit'/, не́бо /nébə/, о́блако /óblakə/, хорошо́ /hərashó/, молоко́ /məlakó/.

In syllables before a stress, **e** and **я** are pronounced as "ee" /i/ as in English **tree, see**. Петербу́рг /pitirburk/, телефо́н /tilifón/, телегра́мма /tiligrámma/, сестра́ /sistrá/, рестора́н /ristarán/, звезда́ /zvizdá/, язы́к /yizýk/. In syllables after the stress they are pronounced closer to the sound of the "i" in English **h**i**t, **i**t, y**i**p /i/: де́вять /devit'/, де́сять /désit'/, ве́тер /vétir/.

Like vowels, consonants in Russian also undergo certain changes following the rules outlined below.

1. In the final position any voiced consonant automatically becomes voiceless in the final position: друг /druk/, клуб/ klup/, сад /sat/, моро́з /marós/, снег /snek/.
If a final consonant is already voiceless, no changes occur: парк/park/, суп /sup/.
Sonorants (consonants that can only be voiced: л, м, н, р) never undergo any changes: пол /pol/, дом /dom/, сон /son/, бар /bar.

2. In two-consonant clusters where one consonant is voiced and the other voiceless, it is the second consonant that will influence the first and make it similar. This phenomenon is called consonant assimilation. The following are examples of the first consonant in a cluster becoming devoiced because it is followed by a voiceless consonant: во́дка /votkə/, ска́зка /skaskə/,

книжка /knishkə/, ложка /loshkə/. The opposite process occurs when the second consonant of a cluster is voiced: футбол /fudbol/, сделать /zdelət'/, просьба /proz'bə/. The cluster /св/ is an exception; it is called "inert" because it never undergoes any changes: свадьба /svad'bə/, до свидания /dəsvidaniyə/.

Remember that prepositions are always pronounced together with the word that they preceed and therefore also form consonant clusters and are subject to the same rules: в доме /vdómi/, в парке /fpárki/, из леса /izlésə/, из театра /istiátrə/.

3. Special attention should be paid to the pronunciation of "soft" (palatalized) consonants. Remember that palatalization/softening in Russian occurs if a consonant is followed by a soft sign or any of the following vowels: я, е, ю, и, and ё. This is true for all consonants except ж, ш, and ц, which always remain hard.

An example of a "hard" or non-palatalized consonant in English is the sound of /l/ in *look*. Here /l/ is considered a hard sound. Compare this to the sound of /l/ in *flute* or *prelude*, and you will notice the difference. The second examples illustrate what in Russian is referred to as a "soft" or palatalized consonant. Palatalized consonants are so called because when we pronounce them, our tongue stays on the palate longer.

Another difference between hard and soft consonants can be observed in comparing the English pronunciation of /n/ in *canon* (a "hard" or non-palatalized /n/) and *canyon* (a "soft" or palatalized

/n/). If we compare the English word *net* /net/ and the Russian word for "no," нет /n'et/,

consisting of the same letters, we will see that the Russian /n/ sound is "soft" or palatalized.

Let's look at some Russian examples: любо́вь contains two palatalized consonants, л and в,

devoiced in the final position to /f'/; смерть contains two palatalized consonants, м and т; кровь

contains one palatalized consonant, в, devoiced at the final position to /f'/.

Let's observe how these rules of pronunciation work together in a poetic text.

Below is Lermontov's poem "Па́рус," accompanied by a phonetic guide for its pronunciation.

You can also listen to it on the companion website. As you listen to it and read it aloud, pay

special attention to the vowel reductions of unstressed o's and e's. In addition to the vowel

reductions, note how the preposition в is devoiced in the combinations "в тума́не," "в стране́,"

and "в краю́" because of the consonant cluster rule discussed above.

Беле́ет па́рус одино́кой
/bilе́yit pа́rus adinо́kəi/

В тума́не мо́ря голубо́м.
/ftumа́ni mо́r'a gəlubо́m/

Что и́щет он в стране́ далёкой?
/shtə ischit on fstranе́ dal'о́kəi/

Что ки́нул он в краю́ родно́м?
/shtə kі́nul on fkrayу́ radnо́m?/

Игра́ют во́лны, ве́тер сви́щет,
/igrа́yut vо́lny, vе́tir svі́schit,

И ма́чта гнётся и скрыпи́т.
/i mа́chtə gnyо́tsə i skripі́t/

Увы́! Он сча́стия не и́щет,

/uvy on schástiyə ni ischit/

И не от счáстия бежúт.
/i ni atschástiyə bizhhit/

Под нúм струя́ светлéй лазýри,
/padnim struyá svitléi lazuri/

Над нúм луч сóлнца золотóй. . .
/nadnim luch sólncə zəlatói/

А он, мятéжный, прóсит бýри,
/aón, mitézhnyi, prósit buri/

Как бýдто в бýрях éсть покóй.
/kagbuttə vbureh yést' pakói/

After this brief overview of the rules of Russian pronunciation you are ready to put them in

practice and begin your journey into the beautiful and magical world of Russian poetry.

List of Abbreviations
(Список условных сокращений)

adj. – adjective
adv. – adverb
arch. – archaic
auth. – authorly; usage unique to this author
colloq. – colloquial
comp. – comparative
conv. – conversational
dim. – diminutive form
eccl. – ecclesiastical
f. – feminine
fig. – figurative
Fr. – French
idiom. – idiomatic
Impf. – Imperfective
кр. (краткая форма) – short form
n. - neuter
m. – masculine
 sg. – singular
syn. – synonym
см. (смотрите) – see
Perf. – Perfective
pl. – plural
poet. – poetic

Nom. – Именительный падеж – Nominative case
Gen. – Родительный падеж – Genitive case
D. – Дательный падеж – Dative case
Acc. – Винительный падеж – Accusative case
Instr. – Творительный падеж – Instrumental case
Prep. – Предложный падеж – Prepositional case

Алекса́ндр Серге́евич Пу́шкин (1799–1837)

Alexander Pushkin is considered the greatest Russian poet, and the founder of the contemporary Russian literary language. He was born in Moscow into a noble family. Among his ancestors was a captive Abyssinian who became the personal servant and then a protégé of Tsar Peter the Great, and Pushkin subsequently wrote about his great-grandfather in his unfinished novel, *Ара́п Петра́ Вели́кого.*

Pushkin received an excellent education at the Lycée at Tsarskoe Selo, near St. Petersburg, an exclusive boarding school established by Alexander I for the sons of noble families. His talent as a poet was already evident during his early years at the lycée, where he wrote poems in both Russian and French. While there, Pushkin was asked to recite one of his poems before the celebrated Russian poet Gavriil Derzhavin, and Derzhavin was so impressed with the talent of the young poet that he hailed him as his successor. Later Pushkin wrote about this meeting:

"Стари́к Держа́вин нас заме́тил / И в гроб сходя́, благослови́л" (The old Derzhavin noticed us/ and entering his grave, he blessed us). The years spent at the lycée were very happy ones for Pushkin. Throughout his life he maintained friendships with his close lycée friends Ivan Puschin, Anton Del'vig, and Wilhelm Küchelbecker, and he wrote many poems reflecting on his time at Tsarskoe Selo. His famous poem "19 октября," written in 1825, was dedicated to the anniversary of the opening of the lycée in 1811.

Друзья́ мои, прекра́сен наш сою́з!	My friends, our union is beatiful!
Он как душа́ неразделим и ве́чен –	It is, like the soul, indivisible and eternal –
Неколеби́м, свобо́ден и беспе́чен	Steadfast, free and carefree
Сраста́лся он под се́нью дру́жных муз.	It grew in the shelter of friendly muses
Куда́ бы нас ни бро́сила судьби́на,	No matter where fate might cast us
И сча́стие куда́ б ни повело́,	And wherever fortune might lead us
Всё те же мы: нам це́лый мир чужби́на;	We are still the same; the whole world is a foreign land for us
Оте́чество нам Ца́рское Село́.	Our fatherland is Tsarskoe Selo.

After graduating from the lycée, Pushkin was given a position at the Collegium of Foreign Affairs in St. Petersburg. For three years he led a carefree life immersed in Petersburg society and its diversions. In this period he wrote many romantic poems influenced by Byron, and in 1820 he published his first long poem, "Ruslan and Ludmila." Some of his poetry seemed too liberal for Tsar Alexander I, and Pushkin was transferred from St. Petersburg to the south of Russia, first to Kishinev in Moldova and then to Odessa, where he spent the years 1820–1824. This period is known as the Romantic period in Pushkin's poetry. At that time he wrote his long poems "The Prisoner of the Caucasus" (Кавка́зский пле́нник), "The Fountain of Bakhchisarai" (Бахчисара́йский фонта́н), and "The Robber Brothers" (Бра́тья Разбо́йники), of which only fragments remain, and he began "The Gypsies" (Цыга́ны).

While in Odessa, Pushkin fell in love with Yelizaveta Vorontsova, the wife of Count Vorontsov, who was the governor of the region at that time and stationed in Odessa. The relationship between Puhskin and Count Vorontsov, who was his supervisor, was difficult from the beginning, and Vorontsov's jealousy made it all the more acrimonious. Vorontsov began to persecute Pushkin, and Pushkin offered his resignation. Finally, after the censors intercepted one of Pushkin's letters, in which he wrote about his interest in "atheist teachings" (for more, see Yuri Lotman's biography of Pushkin), he was dismissed from service in Vorontsov's office and exiled to his estate, Mikhailovskoe, near Pskov, where he spent 1824–1826. There he wrote "Boris Godunov"; continued to work on "The Gypsies" and *Eugene Onegin*; and wrote many love poems, among which is the famous "Я по́мню чу́дное мгнове́нье…," dedicated to Anna Kern, who was visiting her aunt (and Pushkin's neighbor and friend) Praskovia Osipova at the nearby estate of Trigorskoe. In the evenings Pushkin listened to the many folktales of his nanny, Arina Rodionovna, who became the prototype of Tatyana's nanny in *Eugene Onegin*. Pushkin's poem "Зи́мний ве́чер" describes one of those evenings.

After the Decembrist revolt of 1825, in which many of Pushkin's friends were involved, Pushkin was brought by convoy from Mikhailovskoe to Moscow to meet the new tsar, Nikolai I, who promised Pushkin "forgiveness" and assured him that he was going to be his personal censor, but throughout Pushkin's life there were still many sunsequent clashes with censorship. Pushkin hoped that the new tsar would bring long-awaited reforms to Russia, but these hopes were not fulfilled.

In 1826 Pushkin wrote "Посла́ние в Сиби́рь" (Letter to Siberia), which he addressed to his Decembrist friends sentenced to hard labor in the Siberian mines, and Maria Volkonskaya took the poem with her as she prepared to join her exiled husband in Siberia. During this period Pushkin's interest in Russian history deepened, and he wrote the long poem "Полта́ва" (Poltava) and the novel *Ара́п Петра́ Вели́кого,* which remained unfinished. At this time he also became friends with a celebrated Polish poet, Adam Mickiewicz, who was in exile in Russia.

In 1829 Pushkin met sixteen-year-old Natalya Goncharova, who was considered the most beautiful woman in Russia. He proposed to her but was not accepted at first; Natalya and her family wanted to be sure that Pushkin's troubles with the government had been resolved and that his position was stable, so only in 1830, after his second proposal, did Pushkin and Natalya Goncharova become engaged. After the engagement, in the autumn of 1830 Pushkin went to the family estate of Boldino on business but was forced to remain there for several months because of a cholera epidemic in Moscow. This period in Pushkin's life later became known as Бо́лдинская о́сень (the Boldino autumn) because of its rich creative legacy. In Boldino Pushkin finished *Eugene Onegin* and wrote four "little tragedies" ("Ма́ленькие траге́дии") in verse and a cycle of short stories, *The Tales of Belkin* ("По́вести Бе́лкина").

In 1831 after a long courtship Pushkin married Natalya Goncharova. Her beauty attracted the attention of the tsar, who awarded Pushkin the title of *Kammerjunker,* a very low court title usually bestowed upon young officers, so that his wife could regularly attend the court balls.

Pushkin was offended; he felt that this low rank was inappropriate for his age and reflected Nikolai I's opinion that poets were not of very high status in society. Court life with its balls and receptions held no interest for Pushkin, and he felt that at court he had less time for poetry. Natalya's beauty sparked the interest of a French baron, Georges d'Anthès, who started to pursue her. Pushkin challenged d'Anthès to a duel; fortunately the first scheduled duel was averted because d'Anthès married Natalya's sister, Yekaterina, claiming that he was in love with her and not with Natalya. But the rumors about him and Pushkin's wife continued to circulate, and eventually Pushkin recived an anonymous letter congratulating him on "having joined the order of cuckolds." A second duel was scheduled and took place on January 27, 1837. Two days later Pushkin died of a stomach wound in his apartment near the Moika River in St. Petersburg. He is buried beside his mother in the Svyatogorsk Monastery cemetery near his family estate of Mikhailovskoe.

Although Pushkin's life was tragically cut short by his death at the age of thirty-seven because of the duel over the honor of his wife, he left a very rich and influential literary legacy. He worked in all literary genres—from poems to fairy tales to historic chronicles to plays to his innovative "novel in verse" (рома́н в стиха́х) *Eugene Onegin*. When Pushkin died, the celebrated Russian literary critic Vissarion Belinsky said of him: "Со́лнце ру́сской поэзии закати́лось" (The sun of Russian poetry has gone down). Pushkin's birthday, June 6, is celebrated as a holiday in Russia and is known as Пу́шкинский День Росси́и.

Зо́лото и Була́т * (1814, опубл. 1827)

"Всё моё," – сказа́ло **зла́то**;   зла́то *(arch., poet)* – зо́лото – gold

"Всё моё," – сказа́л **була́т**.   була́т *(arch., poet.)* – меч – sword

"Всё куплю́," – сказа́ло зла́то;

"Всё возьму́," – сказа́л була́т.

Лексика и грамматика

1. What tenses and aspects are used for the verbs in the poem? List all the verbs, indicating their aspect and tense.

_____

_____

2. Find all the usages of the pronoun "всё" in this poem. Indentify the case and the governing verb (if present) in each instance.

_____

3. Find the verbs that are in the first person and provide the infinitive forms for these verbs.

_____

Вопросы для обсуждения

1. What is the argument between the gold and the sword?

2. How do you understand the opposition that the poet sets up?

3. Which do you think is more powerful? Explain your point of view.

Róза * (1815)

Друзья́ мой!

Увя́ла ро́за,   увя́нуть *(Perf.)* – to wilt, die off

Дитя́ **зари́**! . . .   заря́ – dawn

Не говори́:

Вот жи́зни мла́дость,

Не **повтори́**:   повтори́ть *(Perf.)* – to repeat

Так вя́нет ра́дость,   вя́нуть *(Impf.)* – to wilt, wither; ра́дость *(f.)* – joy

В **душе́** скажи́:   душа́ – soul

Прости́! жале́ю. . . .   прости́ть *(Perf.)* – to forgive; жале́ть *(Impf.)* – to be sorry

И на **лиле́ю**   лиле́я *(arch., poet.)* – ли́лия – lily

Нам **укажи́.**   указа́ть *(Perf.)* (кому на что) – to point out

Лексика и грамматика

1. "Жить" means "to live." What is the meaning of "жизнь" in English?_____

What is the shared root? _____

2. "Де́ти" means "children." What is the meaning of "дитя́" in English?_____

What is the shared root? _____

3. To what in the poem does "дитя́ зари́" refer in the first stanza? _____

Why does the poet describe it like that? _____

4. Find the verbs in the imperative mood._____

5. Find the verbs in the Perfective aspect and explain the aspectual choice.

_____

6. Find the verbs in the Imperfective aspect and explain the aspectual choice.

_____

Вопросы для обсуждения

1. What is the mood of the poem?

2. How can the metaphor of the rose and the lily be understood?

Я вас люби́л . . . * (1829)

This poem is dedicated to Anna Olenina, the pretty and well-educated youngest daughter of Alexei Olenin, the president of the St. Petersburg Academy of Fine Arts. Pushkin was in love with Anna in 1828–1829 and even proposed marriage, but his proposal was not accepted by her family because he was not considered a good match for Anna. Pushkin dedicated several poems to Olenina, some of which—"Ты и Вы," "Не пой, краса́вица, при мне . . ."—are in this book. As it became known later from her diary, Anna at the time was unhappily in love with Alexei Lobanov-Rostovsky and was indifferent to Pushkin.

Я вас люби́л: любо́вь **ещё, быть мо́жет,**   ещё – still; быть мо́жет – may be

В **душе́** мое́й **уга́сла** не **совсе́м;**   душа́ – soul; уга́снуть *(Perf.)* – to be extinguished; совсе́м – fully

Но **пусть** она́ вас **бо́льше не трево́жит;** пусть – let; бо́льше не – no longer; трево́жить *(Impf.)* – to trouble

Я не хочу́ **печа́лить** вас **ниче́м.**   печа́лить *(Impf.)* – to sadden; ниче́м – not by anything *(Instr.* of ничто)

Я вас люби́л **безмо́лвно, безнаде́жно,**   безмо́лвно – wordlessly; безнаде́жно – hopelessly

То ро́бостью, то ре́вностью томи́м;   By shyness and by jealousy tormented

Я вас люби́л так **и́скренно,** так **не́жно,**   и́скренно – sincerely; не́жно – tenderly

Как дай вам Бог люби́мой быть други́м. As may God grant you be loved by someone else

Лексика и грамматика

1. What do you think "любо́вь" means in English?_____

2. "Печа́лить" means "to sadden." What is the meaning of "печа́ль" in English?_____
_____. What is the root that the noun and the verb share?_____

2. Find all the usages of the pronoun "вас" in this poem. What case is being used?

_____. Identify the governing verbs in each instance._____

3. To which word in the poem does "она́" refer in the first stanza?_____

4. Find the words "безмо́лвно" and "безнаде́жно." What do you think the prefix "без–" means?

_____

5. Find all the adverbs in the poem. _____

6. Find all the uses of the Instrumental case. _____

Вопросы для обсуждения

1. What is the tone of the poem?

2. Are the poet's feelings reciprocated?

3. Does the poet still love her?

Ты и Вы * (1828)

This poem is dedicated to Anna Olenina, who once misspoke by saying *ты* to Pushkin; the following Sunday he brought her the poem. In standard Russian, *вы* is used as the appropriate form of address between adults. Even now, in contemporary standard usage, the more intimate *ты* is reserved for family, very close friends, lovers, and God. In the nineteenth century it was used even more rarely, and even children of the upper classes were expected to address their parents as *вы*.

Пусто́е *вы* **серде́чным** *ты*	пусто́й – empty; серде́чный – heartfelt
Она́, обмо́лвясь, замени́ла	обмо́лвиться – to let slip; замени́ть – to replace

9

И всё счастли́вые **мечты́**	мечта́ – dream
В **душе́** влюблённой **возбуди́ла**.	душа́ – soul; возбуди́ть – to arouse, awake
Пред не́й **заду́мчиво** стою́,	пред *(Instr.)* – in front of; заду́мчивый – pensive
Свести́ оче́й с неё нет си́лы;	I can't take my eyes off her
И говорю́ ей: как *вы* **ми́лы**!	мил, мила́, ми́ло, ми́лы – sweet, nice
И **мы́слю**: как *тебя́* люблю́!	мы́слить – ду́мать

Лексика и грамматика

1. "Люби́ть" means "to love." What is the meaning of "влюблённый" in English? _____. What is the root that the verb and the participle share? _____

2. Find all the personal pronouns in the poem. _____

Identify their cases and the governing verbs in each instance._____

_____

3. Find the word "заду́мчиво." Can you name the verb to which this adverb is related? _____. What is their common root? _____

4. Find all the uses of the Accusative case. _____

5. Find all the uses of the Instrumental case. _____

Вопросы для обсуждения

1. What happened in the conversation between the poet and his beloved?

2. How does he react to her slip of the tongue?

3. How is the shift between *ты* and *вы* played out in the poem?

Не пой, краса́вица, при мне . . .* (1828)

This poem was inspired by Anna Olenina (see the note above for "Я вас люби́л"), who was known for her musical talents as a singer and composer. The Russian composer Sergey Rachmaninov set this poem to music in 1893.

Не **пой, краса́вица, при** мне́	пой – *Impf.* of петь; краса́вица – beauty; при – in front of
Ты **пе́сен Гру́зии печа́льной:**	пе́сня – song; Гру́зия – Georgia; печа́льный – sad
Напомина́ют мне **оне́**	напомина́ть (кому) – to remind; оне́ *(arch.)* – они
Другу́ю жизнь и **бе́рег да́льный**.	друго́й – another; бе́рег – shore; да́льный – distant, faraway

Увы́! напомина́ют мне	увы́ – alas
Твои́ **жесто́кие напе́вы**	жесто́кий – cruel; напе́в – melody
И **степь**, и ночь – и при луне́	степь *(f.)* – steppe
Черты́ далёкой, бе́дной **де́вы.**	черта́ – *here:* feature; де́ва – maiden

Я **при́зрак ми́лый, роково́й,**	при́зрак – phantom; роково́й – fatal
Тебя́ **уви́дев**, забыва́ю;	уви́дев –past participle of уви́деть
Но ты поёшь – и **предо мно́й**	предо мно́й – before me
Его́ я вновь вообража́ю.	вообража́ть *(Impf.)* – to imagine

Не пой, краса́вица, при мне́
Ты пе́сен Гру́зии печа́льной:
Напомина́ют мне оне́
Другу́ю жизнь и бе́рег да́льный.

Лексика и грамматика

1. "Петь" means "to sing." Find the common root in петь – напéв – пéсня.

_____

List other words with the same root._____

2. "Напоминáть" means "to remind." Find the common root in напоминáть – пóмнить –

пáмять – воспоминáния. _____

Write down other words with the same root._____

3. What is the case of "онé" in the third line of the first stanza? _____

4. In the first stanza the pronoun "мне" appears twice. What case is being used in each instance?

Indicate the governing verb. _____

5. In the third stanza what case is used for "прúзрак"? _____

6. To what does the pronoun "его" refer in the third stanza? _____

7. Find all the adjectives in this poem (8). _____

_____

Can you find the two that are synonyms? _____. What is the

shared root? _____

Вопросы для обсуждения

1. What are the main emotions in the poem?

2. What feeling does the landscape in the second stanza evoke?

3. Why is Georgia called "sad"?

4. How does the poem begin?

5. What is the link between music and memory?

6. The poet refers to his past love as "при́зрак ми́лый, роково́й." What can we infer about the nature of their relationship? Was it a happy one?

7. Why do you think the last stanza repeats the first?

На хо́лмах Гру́зии . . . * (1829)

This poem, like the previous one, was written during Pushkin's journey to Georgia, which he first visited in 1824 during his southern exile. The images of exotic mountains and nature in the Caucasus were also very appealing to Lermontov and other Russian poets of the Romantic era.

На **хо́лмах Гру́зии** лежи́т ночна́я **мгла́**;   холм – hill; Гру́зия – Georgia; мгла – darkness

    Шуми́т **Ара́гва** пре́до мно́ю.   Ара́гва – river in Georgia

Мне гру́стно и легко́; **печа́ль моя́ светла́**;   печа́ль *(f.)* – sadness; све́тлый – light

    Печа́ль моя́ **полна́** тобо́ю,   полна́ – *cf.* по́лный – full

Тобо́й, одно́й тобо́й . . . **Уны́нья** моего́   уны́нье – melancholy

    Ничто́ не **му́чит**, не **трево́жит**,   му́чить *(Impf.)* – to torment; трево́жить – to trouble

И **се́рдце** вновь **гори́т** и лю́бит – **оттого́**,   се́рдце – heart; горе́ть *(Imprf.)* – to burn

    Что не люби́ть оно́ не мо́жет.   оттого́ – *here:* because

Лексика и грамматика

1. "Шум" means "noise." What do you think "шуме́ть" means in English?_____

What is the aspect of this verb? _____. Make up a sentence with this

verb._____

2. "Но́вый" means "new." What does the adverb "вновь" mean?_____

3. Find all the usages of the pronoun "тобо́й" in this poem. What case is being used?

_____

4. What case is used in the fifth line for "Уны́нья"? _____. What is the subject

of that sentence?_____

5. To which word in the poem does "оно́" refer in the last line?_____

6. Of how many sentences does the poem consist? _____

Identify them by reading each sentence aloud.

7. Find all the adverbs in the poem. _____

Вопросы для обсуждения

1. What is the mood of the poem?

2. How do you understand the words "печа́ль моя́ светла́"? Why does the poet describe his sadness as "light"?

3. What are the main emotions in the poem?

У́зник ** (1822)

Significantly, this poem was written while Pushkin was in exile in the south of Russia in the Crimea for his satirical epigrams against the Russian emperor and some highly placed officials.

Сижу́ за **решёткой в темни́це сыро́й**.	решётка – bar; темни́ца – prison; сыро́й – damp
Вскормлённый в нево́ле орёл молодо́й,	вскормлённый в нево́ле – raised in captivity; орёл – eagle
Мой гру́стный това́рищ, **маха́я крыло́м**.	маха́ть – to flap; крыло́ – wing
Крова́вую пи́щу клюёт под окно́м,	крова́вый – bloody; пи́ща – food; клева́ть – to peck
Клюёт, и **броса́ет**, и смо́трит в окно́,	броса́ть – *here:* to stop
Как бу́дто со мно́ю **заду́мал** одно́;	как бу́дто – as if; заду́мать – to think up

14

Зовёт меня **взгля́дом** и **кри́ком** свои́м   взгляд – look; крик – screech

И **вы́молвить** хо́чет: "Дава́й **улети́м**!   вы́молвить – to utter; улете́ть – to fly away

Мы **во́льные пти́цы**; **пора́**, брат, пора́!   во́льный – free; пти́ца – bird; пора́ – it's time

Туда́, где за **ту́чей** беле́ет **гора́**,   ту́ча – storm cloud; гора́ – mountain

Туда́, где сине́ют **морски́е края́**,   морско́й – sea; край – edge

Туда́, где гуля́ем **лишь ве́тер** . . . **да я**!..."   лишь – only; ве́тер – wind; да *(colloq.)* – and

Лексика и грамматика

1. "Нево́ля" and "во́льный" share a common root. Find the root and write down its meaning in English. _____

2. The verb "беле́ть" is derived from "бе́лый" (white). Can you guess the meaning of the verb?
_____

"Сине́ть" is similarly formed from "си́ний" (dark blue). Write down the meaning of the verb in English. Using the same model, can you come up with any other examples of verbs denoting color? _____

3. List all the examples of the Instrumental case (5). _____

_____

4. Find the common root in улете́ть – самолёт – лета́ть – полёт – прилете́ть and write down its

meaning in English. _____. Make up two sentences with these words.

_____

_____

1. What is the mood of the poem?

2. How does it change from the first to the third stanza?

3. Where does the eagle call the lyric hero?

4. What oppositions are set up in the poem?

Зимняя доро́га ** (1826)

Сквозь волни́стые тума́ны	Through undulating fogs
Пробира́ется луна́,	пробира́ться – to make one's way through; луна́ – moon
На печа́льные **поля́ны**	поля́на – glade
Льёт печа́льно **свет** она́.	лить – to pour; свет – light
По доро́ге зи́мней, ску́чной	
Тро́йка **бо́рзая** бежи́т,	бо́рзый (*arch.*, in reference to a horse) – gallant
Колоко́льчик однозву́чный	колоко́льчик – bell; однозву́чный – monotonous
Утоми́тельно греми́т.	утоми́тельный – tiring; греме́ть – to ring
Что-то слы́шится **родно́е**	родно́й – familiar, dear
В до́лгих пе́снях **ямщика́:**	ямщи́к – coachman
То **разгу́лье удало́е,**	разгу́лье – revelry; удало́й – *here:* spirited, bold
То серде́чная **тоска́** . . .	тоска́ – sadness, melancholy

Ни огня́, ни чёрной **ха́ты**,   ха́та – hut

Глушь и снег.... Навстре́чу мне   глушь *(f.)* – depth of the country

То́лько **вёрсты полоса́ты**   верста́ *(arch.)* – a marker of distance (0.662 mile);

 полоса́тый – striped

Попада́ются одне́ ...   попада́ться – to come up; одне́ *(arch.)* – одни́

Ску́чно, гру́стно ... за́втра, Ни́на,

За́втра к ми́лой **возвратя́сь**,   возвратя́сь – having returned

Я забу́дусь у **ками́на**,   забы́ться – to lose oneself (as in reverie); ками́н – fireplace

Загляжу́сь не наглядя́сь.   I will feast my eyes on you, unable to look my fill

Зву́чно стре́лка часова́я   зву́чно – audibly; стре́лка –hand (of the clock)

Ме́рный круг свой **соверши́т,**   ме́рный – measured; круг – circle; соверши́тъ – to complete

И, **доку́чных удаля́я,**   доку́чные – *here:* bothersome people; удаля́я – having removed

По́лночь нас не **разлучи́т.**   разлучи́ть – to separate

Гру́стно, Ни́на: путь мой ску́чен,

Дре́мля смо́лкнул мой ямщи́к,   дре́мля – having dozed off; смо́лкнутъ – to fall silent

Колоко́льчик однозву́чен,

Отума́нен лу́нный **лик.**   отума́нен – foggy; лик *(arch.)* – лицо́

17

Лексика и грамматика

1. "Туман" means "fog." Find the root in "отума́нен." Make up a sentence with this word.

_____

2. Find two roots in "однозву́чный" and write down their meanings in English.

_____

3. List all the adjectives in the poem._____

4. What tense and aspect are used in the first four stanzas?_____

5. What tense and aspect are used in the fifth and sixth stanzas? Why does the tense change?

_____

Вопросы для обсуждения

1. What is the atmosphere of the poem?

2. Describe the winter landscape.

3. Where is the poet going?

4. Who is Nina?

5. What are his hopes for the following day?

Зи́мний ве́чер ** (1825)

This poem was inspired by the long winter evenings that Pushkin spent at Mikhailovskoe listening to the tales of his old nanny, Arina Rodionovna.

Бу́ря мгло́ю не́бо **кро́ет,**	бу́ря – storm; мгла – darkness; крыть *(Impf.)* – to cover
Ви́хри снѐжные **крутя́;**	ви́хрь – swirl; крутя́ –whirling
То, как зве́рь, она **заво́ет,**	то . . . то – now . . . then; зве́рь – beast; завы́ть *(Perf.)* – to howl

18

То **запла́чет**, как **дитя́**,	запла́кать *(Perf.)* – to cry; дитя́ *(arch.)* – baby
То по **кро́вле обветша́лой**	кро́вля *(arch.)* – roof; обветша́лый – decrepit
Вдруг соло́мой зашуми́т,	вдруг – suddenly; соло́ма – straw; зашуме́ть *(Perf.)* – to make noise;
То, как **пу́тник запозда́лый**,	пу́тник – traveler; запозда́лый – late
К нам в **око́шко застучи́т**.	око́шко *(dim.)* – window; застуча́ть *(Perf.)* – to knock
На́ша **ве́тхая лачу́жка**	ве́тхий – *here:* old, run down; лачу́жка *(dim.)* – cabin
И печа́льна и **темна́**.	темна́ – *cf.* тёмный – dark
Что же ты́, моя́ стару́шка,	
Приумо́лкла у окна́?	приумо́лкнуть *(Perf.)* – to grow silent
Или бу́ри **завыва́ньем**	завыва́нье – howling
Ты, мой друг, **утомлена́**,	утомлена́ – *cf.* утомлённый – weary
Или **дре́млешь** под **жужжа́ньем**	дрема́ть *(Impf.)* – to doze; жужжа́нье – humming
Своего́ **веретена́**?	веретено́ – spindle
Вы́пьем, до́брая подру́жка	вы́пить *(Perf.)* – *here:* to have a drink
Бе́дной **ю́ности** мое́й,	ю́ность *(f.)* – youth
Вы́пьем с го́ря; где же **кру́жка**?	вы́пить с го́ря *(idiom.)* – to drown one's sorrows; кру́жка – mug
Се́рдцу бу́дет веселе́й.	се́рдце – heart
Спой мне пе́сню, как **сини́ца**	сини́ца – chickadee
Ти́хо за́ морем жила́;	ти́хо – quietly; за́ морем – *here:* oversees

Спой мне пе́сню, как **деви́ца**   деви́ца – maiden

За водо́й **поутру** шла.   поутру *(colloq., arch.)* – in the morning

Бу́ря мгло́ю не́бо кро́ет,

Ви́хри сне́жные крутя́;

То, как зверь, она́ заво́ет,

То запла́чет, как дитя́.

Вы́пьем, до́брая подру́жка

Бе́дной ю́ности мое́й,

Вы́пьем с го́ря; где же кру́жка?

Се́рдцу бу́дет веселе́й.

Лексика и грамматика

1. Find the root in "запозда́лый" and write down its meaning in English. _____

List other words with the same root. _____

_____

2. Find the root in "зашуме́ть" and write down its meaning in English._____

List other words with the same root._____

_____

3. Путь – пу́тник – спу́тник share a common root. Find the root and give its meaning in English.

_____. Make up a sentence with any of these words.

_____

20

4. Приумо́лкнуть – смо́лкнуть – молча́ть – молча́ние share a common root. Find the root and write down its meaning in English. _____. Make up two sentences with any of these words._____

_____

5. Обветша́лый – ве́тхий share a common root. Find the root and write down its meaning in English._____. Make up a sentence with any of these words.

_____

6. List all the verbs in the Perfective aspect (7). _____

_____

_____

Make up two sentences with any of these verbs.

_____

_____

Вопросы для обсуждения

1. How is the winter evening described in the poem?

2. What is the atmosphere of the poem?

3. How is the storm personified? Find specific examples in the text.

4. Whom does the poet call "До́брая подру́жка бе́дной ю́ности мое́й"?

Зи́мнее у́тро ** (1829)

Моро́з и со́лнце; день **чуде́сный**!   моро́з – frost; чуде́сный – marvelous

Ещё ты **дре́млешь**, друг **преле́стный** –	дрема́ть – to doze; преле́стный – lovely
Пора́, краса́вица, **просни́сь**:	просну́ться – to wake up
Откро́й **сомкну́ты не́гой взо́ры**	сомкну́ты – *here:* closed; не́га – bliss; взо́ры – *here:* eyes
Навстре́чу се́верной Авро́ры,	навстре́чу – toward; Авро́ра – Aurora, goddess of the dawn
Звездо́ю се́вера яви́сь!	звезда́ – star; се́вер –north; яви́ться – to appear
Вечо́р, ты по́мнишь, **вью́га зли́лась**,	вечо́р *(arch.)* – last night; вью́га – blizzard; зли́ться – to rage
На **му́тном** не́бе **мгла носи́лась**;	му́тный – cloudy; мгла – darkness; носи́ться – to rush
Луна́, как **бле́дное пятно́**,	бле́дный – pale; пятно́ – spot
Сквозь **ту́чи мра́чные** желте́ла,	ту́ча – storm cloud; мра́чный – gloomy
И ты печа́льная сиде́ла –	
А **ны́нче** . . . **погляди́** в окно́:	ны́нче – now; погляде́ть – to take a look
Под голубы́ми **небеса́ми**	небеса́ *(poet.)* – sky
Великоле́пными коврами,	великоле́пный – magnificent; ков/ё/р – carpet
Блестя́ на со́лнце, снег лежи́т;	блестя́ – sparkling
Прозра́чный лес оди́н черне́ет,	прозра́чный – transparent
И **ель** сквозь **и́ней** зелене́ет,	ель – fir tree; и́ней – ice (on the trees)
И ре́чка подо **льдом блести́т**.	лёд – ice; блесте́ть – to sparkle
Вся ко́мната **янта́рным бле́ском**	янта́рный – amber; блеск – radiance

Озарена́. Весёлым **тре́ском**	озарена́ – lit up; треск – crackling
Трещи́т зато́пленная печь.	треща́ть – to crackle; зато́пленный – burning; **печь** – stove
Прия́тно ду́мать у **лежа́нки**.	лежа́нка – sleeping ledge by the stove
Но зна́ешь: не **веле́ть** ли в **са́нки**	веле́ть – order; са́нки *(pl.)* – sleigh
Кобы́лку бу́рую запре́чь?	кобы́лка – mare; бу́рый (in reference to a horse) – brown; запре́чь *(arch.)* – to harness
Скользя́ по у́треннему сне́гу,	скользя́ – gliding
Друг ми́лый, **предади́мся бе́гу**	преда́ться (чему) – to give oneself to; бег – run
Нетерпели́вого коня́	нетерпели́вый – impatient; конь – horse
И **навести́м поля́ пусты́е**,	навести́ть – to visit; по́ле – field; пусто́й – empty
Леса́, неда́вно **столь густы́е**,	столь – *here:* so; густо́й – thick
И **бе́рег**, ми́лый для меня́.	бе́рег – shore

Лексика и грамматика

1. The poet describes a bright winter day as "чуде́сный." What else can be described with this adjective? _____

List other words with the same root. _____

2. In the second and third stanzas find three verbs related to colors and write down their meaning in English.

_____

3. List all the imperatives in the poem. _____

_____

4. Reread the third and fourth stanzas. Can you find two pairs of verbs and nouns that share common roots?

_____

Вопросы для обсуждения:

1. What is the tone of the poem?

2. How does the poet describe the change in the winter landscape? How does the description differ from the night before to the morning? Give specific details. _____

_____

3. What are the main emotions in the poem?_____

Óсень (отры́вок) ** (1833)

Уны́лая пора́! Оче́й очарова́нье!	уны́лый – gloomy; пора́ – time; óчи *(arch.)* – eyes; очарова́нье – enchantment
Прия́тна мне твоя́ **проща́льная краса́** –	проща́льный – *here:* parting; краса́ – beauty
Люблю́ я **пы́шное приро́ды увяда́нье,**	пы́шный – sumptuous; приро́да – nature; увяда́нье – withering
В **багре́ц и в зóлото одéтые леса́,**	багре́ц – crimson; зóлото – gold; одéтый – dressed; лес – woods
В их **сéнях вéтра** шум и **свéжее дыха́нье,**	сéни – *here:* umbrage; вéтер – wind; свéжий – fresh; дыха́нье – breath
И **мглой волни́стою покры́ты** небеса́,	мгла́ – *here:* mist; волни́стый – *here:* sinuous; покры́т – covered

24

И ре́дкий со́лнца **луч**, и пе́рвые **моро́зы,**   луч – ray; моро́з – frost

И отдалённые **седо́й** зимы́ **угро́зы.**   отдалённый – distant; седо́й – gray (in reference to hair

only); гро́за – threat

Лексика и грамматика

1. "Не́бо" means "sky." What do you think "небеса́" means in English?_____ What is the common root? _____

2. "Проща́льный" means "parting." Can you guess the meaning of the verb "проща́ться" с кем/чем?

_____

Make up a sentence with this verb. _____

_____

3. Find the root in "отдалённый." _____ . List other words with the same root

_____

 4. Find all the examples of the Accusative case. _____

5. The adjective "седо́й" describes the color of a person's hair. In your opinion, why does the poet refer to winter as "седа́я"?

Вопросы для обсуждения

1. What is the mood of the poem?

2. How does the poet describe fall?

3. What is special about the combination "оче́й очарова́нье"?

4. What details of the fall landscape are mentioned in the poem?

Я по́мню чу́дное мгнове́нье . . . ** (1825)

This poem reflects an episode from Pushkin's life when he met Anna Kern briefly in St. Peterburg in 1819. She was only eighteen, and Pushkin was struck by her charm and beauty.

They did not see each other for several years after that, but in 1825 they met again when Pushkin was in exile at Mikhailovskoe and Anna was visiting her aunt, who lived nearby. Pushkin fell in love again and wrote her this poem. Later the Russian composer Mikhail Glinka was in love with Anna Kern's daughter Yekaterina, and he set the poem to music in 1840.

Я по́мню **чу́дное мгнове́нье**:	чу́дный – wondrous; мгнове́нье – moment
Передо мной **яви́лась** ты,	яви́ться *(Perf.)* – to appear
Как **мимолётное** виде́нье,	мимолётный – fleeting
Как ге́ний **чи́стой** красоты́.	чи́стый – pure
В **томле́ньях** гру́сти безнаде́жной,	томле́нье – languor
В **трево́гах** шу́мной **суеты́**,	трево́га – *here:* agitation; суета́ – bustle
Звуча́л мне до́лго **го́лос** не́жный	звуча́ть *(Impf.)* – to sound; го́лос – voice
И **сни́лись** ми́лые **черты́**.	сни́ться *(Impf.,* кому) – to appear in a dream; черта́ – feature
Шли го́ды. **Бурь поры́в мяте́жный**	бу́ря – storm; поры́в – gust; мяте́жный – rebellious
Рассе́ял пре́жние мечты́,	рассе́ять *(Perf.)* – to disperse; пре́жний – former
И я забы́л твой го́лос не́жный,	
Твои́ небе́сные черты́.	
В **глуши́**, во **мра́ке заточе́нья**	глушь *(f.)* – depth (of the country); мра́к – gloom; заточе́нье – imprisonment
Тяну́лись ти́хо дни мои́	тяну́ться *(Impf.)* – to stretch, grow long
Без **божества́**, без **вдохнове́нья**,	божество́ – the divine; вдохнове́нье – inspiration
Без **слёз**, без жи́зни, без любви́.	слеза́ – tear

26

Душе́ **наста́ло пробужде́нье:**   наста́ть *(Perf.)* – to come; пробужде́нье – awakening

И вот опя́ть яви́лась ты,

Как мимолётное виде́нье,

Как ге́ний чи́стой красоты́.

И се́рдце бьётся в **упое́нье,**   упое́нье – ecstasy

И для него **воскре́сли** вновь   воскре́снуть *(Perf.)* – to rise again, come back, reawaken

И божество́, и вдохнове́нье,

И жизнь, и слёзы, и любо́вь.

Лексика и грамматика

1. "Мимолётный" consists of two roots. Find them and write down their meanings in English.

_____

What else can be described as "мимолётный"?_____

2. "Наде́жда" means "hope." What is the meaning of "безнаде́жный" in English?_____

 Find the root and the prefix and write down their meanings in English._____

Can you think of any other adjectives with the prefix "без–"?

_____

3. What is the root of "вдохнове́нье"? _____. Can you think of a verb with

the same root?_____

4. To which word in the poem does "для него" refer in the last stanza?_____

5. Find all the neuter nouns in the poem (8)._____

_____

27

6. Find all the uses of the Genitive case (12) and indicate the governing prepositions.

_____

_____

_____

_____

Вопросы для обсуждения

1. What is the mood of the poem?

2. What happened between the poet and his beloved?

3. When did his feelings return?

4. What connection does the poem try to establish between the ability to love and to live life to the fullest?

К Чаада́еву ** (1818)

The philosopher and writer Pyotr Chaadaev (1795–1856) was one of Pushkin's close friends, a prominent figure in Russian high society, a decorated veteran of Russia's war against Napoleon, and a person with close ties to many of the Decembrists. Chaadaev first met Pushkin in 1816 and made a great impression on him. Pushkin addressed three poems to Chaadaev in the epistle genre, and this is the first of them. An epistle poem is written as a letter and addressed to a particular person. The addressee is usually named in the title. This poem was written as a response to an 1818 speech by Alexander I in Warsaw, where he promised the peaceful adoption of a constitution for Russia.

Любви́, наде́жды, **ти́хой сла́вы**	ти́хий – quiet; сла́ва – glory
Недо́лго **не́жил** нас **обма́н,**	не́жить – *here:* coddle; обма́н – deceit
Исче́зли ю́ные заба́вы,	исче́знуть – to disappear; ю́ный – juvenile; заба́ва – amusement

Как сон, как у́тренний тума́н;	тума́н – fog
Но в нас гори́т еще жела́нье,	горе́ть – to burn; жела́нье – desire
Под гнётом вла́сти роково́й	гнёт – oppression; власть – power; роково́й – fatal
Нетерпели́вою душо́й	нетерпели́вый – impatient; душа́ – soul
Отчи́зны вне́млем призыва́нье.	We hear the call of fatherland; внима́ть *(arch.)* – to listen
Мы ждём с томле́ньем упова́нья	томле́нье – yearning; упова́нье *(poet.)* – expectation
Мину́ты во́льности свято́й,	во́льность *(f.)* – freedom; свято́й – sacred
Как ждёт любо́вник молодо́й	любо́вник – lover
Мину́ты ве́рного свида́нья.	ве́рный – *here:* certain; свида́нье – assignation
Пока́ свобо́дою гори́м,	пока́ – as long as
Пока́ сердца́ для че́сти жи́вы,	се́рдце – heart; че́сть *(f.)* – honor
Мой друг, отчи́зне посвяти́м	отчи́зна – fatherland; посвяти́ть *(D.)* – to dedicate
Души́ прекра́сные поры́вы!	поры́в – *here:* outburst
Това́рищ, верь: взойдёт она́,	взойти́ – to rise
Звезда́ плени́тельного сча́стья,	звезда́ – star; плени́тельный – captivating
Росси́я вспря́нет ото сна́,	вспря́нуть *(arch.)* – воспря́нуть – *here:* to rise, wake up; ото – от – from
И на обло́мках самовла́стья	обло́мки *(pl.)* – *here:* remnants; самовла́стье – autocracy
Напи́шут на́ши имена́!	

Лексика и грамматика

1. Find the subject in the opening sentence. _____. What case is used for

"Любви́, наде́жды, ти́хой сла́вы"? _____

2. Find and write down the subject in "но в нас горит ещё желанье."

_____

3. What is the implied subject in "Нетерпеливою душой / Отчизны внемлем призыванье"?

_____

4. Желанье – желать – пожелание share a common root. Find the root and write down its meaning in English. Make up two sentences with these words.

_____

_____

5. "Самовластье" means "autocracy" in English. Find the two roots in Russian and write down their meanings in English. _____

6. Find all the uses of the Instrumental case (4)._____

_____

7. At the end of the poem (fifth line from the bottom) to what does "она" refer? _____

Вопросы для обсуждения

1. What is the main theme of the poem?

2. What does the poet urge his readers to do?

3. What is the mood of the final lines?

Во глубине сибирских руд . . . ** (1827)

This poem was written after the Decembrist revolt on December 25, 1825, in St. Petersburg. Among Pushkin's close friends there were many Decembrists. After the suppression of the revolt, five participants were hanged, and others were exiled to Siberia and sentenced to hard labor. Princess Zinaida Volkonskaya gave a farewell party in her mansion on Tverskaya Street in Moscow in honor of her relative, Maria Volkonskaya, one of the wives of the Decembrists who decided to follow her husband voluntarily to Siberia. Pushkin gave this poem to MariaVolkonskaya, and she brought it to his exiled friends.

Во глубине́ сиби́рских руд	In the depth of the Siberian mines
Храни́те го́рдое терпе́нье,	храни́ть – to keep; го́рдый – proud; терпе́нье – patience
Не **пропадёт** ваш **ско́рбный труд**	пропа́сть – to disappear; ско́рбный – dolorous; труд – labor
И **дум высо́кое стремле́нье.**	ду́ма *(poet.)* – thought; высо́кий – high, lofty; стремле́нье – striving
Несча́стью ве́рная сестра́,	несча́стье – misery; ве́рный – loyal
Наде́жда в **мра́чном подземе́лье**	мра́чный – gloomy; подземе́лье – underground
Разбу́дит бо́дрость и весе́лье,	разбуди́ть – to awaken; бо́дрость *(f.)* – vigor
Придёт **жела́нная пора́:**	жела́нный – long wished for; пора́ – time
Любо́вь и **дру́жество** до вас	дру́жество *(poet.)* – friendship
Дойду́т сквозь мра́чные **затво́ры,**	затво́р *(poet.)* – bar, lock
Как в ва́ши **ка́торжные но́ры**	ка́торжный – *cf.* ка́торга – hard labor; нора́ – hole
Дохо́дит мой свобо́дный **глас.**	глас *(arch.)* го́лос – voice
Око́вы тя́жкие паду́т,	око́вы *(pl.)* – shackles; тя́жкий – heavy; пасть – *here:* to fall off
Темни́цы ру́хнут – и **свобо́да**	темни́ца – prison; ру́хнуть – to collapse; свобо́да – freedom
Вас **при́мет** ра́достно у вхо́да,	приня́ть – to receive
И бра́тья **меч** вам отдаду́т.	меч – sword

Лексика и грамматика

1. "Темни́ца" means prison. Find the root in the word "темни́ца" and write down its meaning in English. _____. Why do you think this particular word is used to describe the prison?

2. Find the root and the prefix in "подземе́лье" and write down their meanings in English.

_____

3. Свобо́да –свобо́дный –освободи́ть share a common root. Find the root and write down its

meaning in English. _____. Make up two sentences with

these words. _____

_____

4. Find all the verbs in the future tense (9) and identify the aspect used. _____

_____

5. Find three verbs of motion and identify their tense, aspect, and meaning: _____

_____

Вопросы для обсуждения

1. What is the theme of the poem?

2. In this letter to his friends what does the poet say about the impact of the Decembrist movement?
Can you find the specific lines in the poem?

3. What future does he envision for his friends?

4. What are the oppositions set up in the poem?

32

Что в и́мени тебе́ моём . . . ** (1830)

Pushkin wrote this poem on January 5, 1830, to a celebrated Polish beauty, Carolina Sobanskaya, who was known for her charm and wit. It was in answer to her request to inscribe his name in her album.

Что в **и́мени** тебе́ моём?	и́мени – (irreg. *Prep.* of и́мя) – name
Оно́ **умрёт**, как **шум** печа́льный	умере́ть *(Perf.)* – to die; шум – noise
Волны́, плесну́вшей в **бе́рег** да́льный,	волна́ – wave; плесну́ть – to splash; бе́рег – shore
Как **звук** ночно́й **в лесу́ глухо́м**.	звук – sound; в лесу́ глухо́м – in the thick forest
Оно́ на **па́мятном листке́**	па́мятный – memorable; лист/о́/к – sheet
Оста́вит **мёртвый след, подо́бный**	мёртвый – dead; след – trace; подо́бный – similar
Узо́ру на́дписи надгро́бной	узо́р – design; на́дпись *(f.)* – inscription; надгро́бный – sepulchral
На непоня́тном языке́.	
Что в нём? **Забы́тое** давно́	забы́тый – forgotten
В **волне́ньях** но́вых и **мяте́жных,**	волне́нье – excitement; мяте́жный – rebellious
Твое́й душе́ не даст оно́	
Воспомина́ний **чи́стых, не́жных**.	чи́стый – pure; не́жный – tender
Но в день печа́ли, в **тишине́,**	тишина́ – quietude
Произнеси́ его́ **тоску́я;**	произнести́ – to utter; тоску́я – with longing

Скажи́: есть па́мять обо мне,   па́мять *(f.)* – memory

Есть в ми́ре се́рдце, где живу́ я . . .   мир – world; се́рдце – heart

Лексика и грамматика

1. "По́мнить" means "to remember." What do you think "воспомина́ние" means in

English?_____. What is the common root? _____. Write down other

words with the same root. _____

2. "Надписа́ть" means "to inscribe." What does "на́дпись" mean? _____

What is the common root? _____. Write down other words with the same root.

_____

3. Find all the usages of the pronoun "оно́" in this poem. To what does it refer? What case is

being used in the first line of the third stanza in "Что в нём?" _____

_____

4. Find all the verbs in the poem. _____

What tense and aspect are used throughout? _____

5. Find all the examples of the Prepositional case in the poem and write them down.

_____

_____

Вопросы для обсуждения

1. What are the main themes of the poem?

2. Whom is the poet addressing?

3. Who is speaking in the last stanza, "есть па́мять обо мне," and what is the final emotion? Is it negative or affirmative? Explain your point of view.

Вакхи́ческая пе́сня *** (1825) вакхи́ческий – bacchanal

Что **смо́лкнул весе́лия глас**?	смо́лкнуть – to grow silent; весе́лье – cheer; глас *(arch.)* – voice
Разда́йтесь, вакха́льны **припе́вы**!	разда́ться – to sound; припе́в – *here:* song
Да здра́вствуют не́жные де́вы	да здра́вствует – long live; не́жный – tender
И ю́ные жёны, люби́вшие на́с!	
Полне́е стака́н налива́йте!	полне́е (*comp.* of по́лный) – full; стака́н – glass
На **зво́нкое дно́**	зво́нкий – resonant; дно́ – bottom
В **густо́е** вино́	густо́й – thick (in reference to liquids only)
Заве́тные ко́льца броса́йте!	заве́тный – cherished; кольцо́ – ring

Поды́мем стака́ны, содви́нем их ра́зом!	подня́ть – to raise; содви́нем их ра́зом – let's clink them at once
Да здра́вствуют **му́зы**, да здра́вствует **ра́зум**!	му́за – muse; ра́зум – reason
Ты, со́лнце **свято́е, гори́**!	свято́й – sacred; горе́ть – to burn, shine
Как э́та **лампа́да бледне́ет**	лампа́да *(arch.)* – lamp; бледне́ть – to pale
Пред я́сным **восхо́дом зари́**,	восхо́д – break; заря́ – dawn
Так **ло́жная му́дрость мерца́ет и тле́ет**	ло́жный – false; му́дрость (*f.*) – wisdom; мерца́ть – to flicker; тле́ть – to smoulder
Пред со́лнцем **бессме́ртным** ума́.	бессме́ртный – immortal

Да здра́вствует со́лнце, да **скро́ется тьма́**! скры́тся – to hide; тьма́ – darkness

Лексика и грамматика

1. What are the five things that the poet celebrates? List them here.

_____

_____

2. Find all the imperatives in the poem. _____

_____

Вопросы для обсуждения

1. What is the mood of the poem?

2. What metaphor is used to describe reason?

3. The poem is written as a toast. What is the purpose of the toast? Indicate the specific lines.

_____

_____

Я па́мятник себе́ воздви́г нерукотво́рный . . . *** (1836)

This poem is a free translation of Horace's Ode XXX, "Exegi monumentum aere perennius. . . ." Horace (65 BC–8 BC) was a leading Roman lyric poet during the reign of Emperor Augustus. In addition to Pushkin, many great Russian poets, such as Lomonosov, Derzhavin, Lermontov, Tyutchev, and Fet, translated Horace's odes. In the final poem of his third book of odes, Horace claimed to have created for himself a monument more durable than bronze. Pushkin used Horace's first line as an epigraph. A celebrated Russian poet of an earlier generation, Gavriil Derzhavin, who met young Pushkin and named him his successor (see Pushkin's biography above), also translated this ode. Thus, Pushkin's interpretation of this poem should be considered in the context not only of Horace but also of Derzhavin, as a poetic testament of sorts stressing the importance of poets and poetry for Russians.

Exegi monumentum (I built a monument)

Я **па́мятник** себе́ **воздви́г нерукотво́рный**,	па́мятник – monument; воздви́гнуть – to construct; нерукотво́рный – not made with human hands
К нему́ не **зарастёт наро́дная тропа́**,	зарасти́ – to become overgrown; наро́дный – people's; тропа́ – path
Вознёсся вы́ше он **главо́ю непоко́рной**	вознести́сь – to rise; глава́ *(poet.)* – head; непоко́рный – defiant
Александри́йского столпа́.	Column in Palace Square in St. Petersburg commemorating Alexander I

Нет, **весь** я не **умру́** – душа́ в **заве́тной ли́ре**	весь – the whole; заве́тный – cherished; ли́ра – lyre
Мой **прах переживёт** и **тле́нья** убежи́т –	прах – *here:* ashes, remains; пережи́ть – to outlive; тле́нье – *here:* decay
И **сла́вен** буду я, **доко́ль** в подлу́нном ми́ре	сла́вен – famous; доко́ль *(arch.)* – as long as; подлу́нный мир *(arch.)* – world
Жив бу́дет **хоть** оди́н **пии́т.**	хоть – only; пии́т *(arch.)* – poet

Слух обо мне́ пройдёт по всей Руси́ **вели́кой**,	слух – rumor; вели́кий – great
И назовёт меня **всяк су́щий** в ней язы́к,	всяк *(arch.)* – any; су́щий – existing
И **го́рдый внук славя́н**, и финн, и **ны́не ди́кой**	го́рдый – proud; внук – grandson; славяни́н – Slav; ны́не *(arch.)* – now; ди́кий – savage

37

Тунгу́с, и друг степе́й калмы́к.	тунгу́с – Tungus, member of an ethnic Siberian group; степь *(f.)* – steppe; калмы́к – a native of Kalmykiya, a southwestern part of Russia on the Caspian Sea.
И до́лго буду тем **любе́зен** я **наро́ду,**	любе́зен – *here:* pleasing; наро́д – people
Что **чу́вства** до́брые я ли́рой **пробужда́л,**	чу́вство – feeling; пробужда́ть – to awaken
Что в мой **жесто́кий век воссла́вил** я Свобо́ду	жесто́кий – cruel; век – century; воссла́вить – to glorify
И **ми́лость** к **па́дшим призыва́л.**	ми́лость *(f.)* – mercy; па́дший – fallen; призыва́ть – to call for
Веле́нью Бо́жию, о му́за, будь **послу́шна,**	веле́нье – will; послу́ш/е/н – obedient
Оби́ды не **страша́сь,** не **тре́буя венца́,**	Not fearing the insult and not demanding the crown
Хвалу́ и **клевету́ прие́мли равноду́шно,**	хвала́ – praise; клевета́ – slander; прие́млеть *(arch.)* – приня́ть – to accept; равноду́шно – indifferently
И не **оспо́ривай глупца́.**	оспо́ривать *(arch.)* – оспа́ривать – to argue (with); глуп/е́/ц – fool

Лексика и грамматика

1. Find the prefix and two roots in "нерукотво́рный" and write down their meanings in English.

_____

2. Па́мятник –па́мять – по́мнить – воспомина́ния share a common root. Find the root and write down its meaning in English. _____. Make up two sentences with these words. _____

_____

3. Find the roots in "равноду́шно" and write down their meanings in English. _____ Make up a sentence with this word. _____

_____

4. Восла́вить – сла́вен – сла́ва share a common root. Find the root and write down its meaning in English. _____. Make up two sentences using these words.

_____

_____

Вопросы для обсуждения

1. What is the main theme of the poem?

2. What kind of a monument is the poet describing?

3. How do you understand the lines "Слух обо мне́ пройдёт по всей Руси́ вели́кой, / И назовёт меня всяк су́щий в ней язы́к, / И го́рдый внук славя́н, и финн, и ны́не ди́кой / тунгу́с и друг степе́й калмы́к"?

4. According to the poem, for what will the poet be remembered?

5. In the poem's conclusion the poet addresses his muse. What does he think the muse ought to do?

Михаи́л Ю́рьевич Ле́рмонтов (1814–1841)

Mikhail Lermontov, fifteen years younger than Pushkin, was the greatest figure of Russian Romanticism. He was born into a rich noble family in Moscow. His mother died from tuberculosis when he was only three years old, and Lermontov was raised by his maternal grandmother on her estate in Tarkhany, about five hundred kilometers south of Moscow in the Penza district. Lermontov's aristocratic grandmother disapproved of her daughter's marriage, which she viewed as a mismatch, and she did not allow Lermontov's father, a poor officer, to participate in the raising of his son. She loved her only grandson very deeply and strove to provide him the best education and every comfort. However, the lifelong feud between his grandmother and his father had a strong negative impact on the personality of the impressionable boy, and later Lermontov wrote an adolescent drama, *People and Passions,* where this quarrel is echoed in the plot.

Little Lermontov was often sick, and at the advice of doctors his grandmother took him to the Caucasus several times during his childhood, hoping that the clear mountain air and mineral springs would improve his frail health. There young Lermontov fell in love with the exotic beauty of the region—its majestic mountains, steep cliffs, and fast rivers—and his great appreciation of this picturesque region stayed with him throughout his life. These early powerful impressions found their artistic reflection in his sketchbooks, paintings, and notebooks.

Lermontov received an excellent education, first at home with foreign tutors, as was customary for the children of the nobility, then at the gymnasium affiliated with Moscow University. Like Pushkin, he was a very precocious and gifted student, and his favorite subject in school was literature. At the age of thirteen Lermontov had already started writing poetry and prose. He was fluent in French and German, and through his English tutor he acquired knowledge of English literature. Lermontov was especially drawn to the works of the great English Romantic poets George Gordon Byron and Percy Bysshe Shelly. He saw many parallels between his own childhood and that of Byron, who was also raised without a father. Young Lermontov also greatly admired the works of Johann Wolfgang von Goethe and Christian Johann Heinrich Heine.

After two years of studies Lermontov left Moscow University and entered the cadet school in St. Petersburg to become an officer in the guards. After graduation he became a frequent visitor at the balls and best salons of St. Petersburg and began to lead the life of leisure and privilege typical of people of his class. His impressions of high society appear in his romantic drama *Masquerade (Маскарáд)* (1835), where the protagonist, Arbenin, is portrayed in sharp contrast to the empty and shallow society. At the end of the play Arbenin goes mad after poisoning his wife, whom he has wrongly accused of infidelity. Because of the difficulties with censorship *Masquerade* was not staged in Lermontov's lifetime, and Lermontov refused to publish it, believing that his play needed to be seen on stage and not merely read. *Masquerade* was staged in parts only in 1852 at the Alexandrinsky Theater in St. Petersburg and the full play finally in 1862.

Shocked by the death of Pushkin, Lermontov wrote a poem, "Death of the Poet" (1837), accusing the tsar's circle of complicity in Pushkin's death. Although not officially published, the poem was copied widely by hand and passed around, and the verses quickly became known. The sixteen searing last lines of the poem, referring to those who were implicated in Pushkin's death as the "executioners of Freedom, Genius and Glory (Вы, жа́дною толпо́й стоя́щие у тро́на, / Свобо́ды, Ге́ния и Сла́вы палачи́!), angered state officials, and Lermontov was sent into exile in the Caucasus as an officer in the dragoons.

When, a year later, after considerable effort by his influential grandmother, Lermontov was pardoned and allowed to return to St. Petersburg, his reputation as a poet grew, and he became a highly sought-after figure in the salons and enjoyed great popularity and fame. He created for himself the reputation of a Don Juan and *bretteur*, and he had a duel with a French officer, Ernest de Barante, over a lady. Since duels were illegal, Lermontov was arrested and sent to the Caucasus again, where he served with great courage and distinction.

Lermontov's great romantic poems *Msyri* (1839) and *Demon* both take place in the mountains of the Caucasus and continue the tradition of European romanticism. Byron's poem "The Prisoner of Chillon," is viewed as an inspiration for Lermontov's *Msyri*. Like Byron, Lermontov structures his poem as a long lyrical monologue by the main hero, Msyri (whose name means "novice" in Georgian), narrating his life. In Lermontov's poem the young hero spent years in a monastery from which he finally escaped and had a brief interval of freedom in the idyllic setting of nature before his death.

Demon is another long romantic poem set in the Caucasus; Lermontov worked on it intermittently for over nine years (1829–1839). In it one can trace a connection to Byron's *Cain* and Milton's *Paradise Lost*. Like these two poets, Lermontov chose to make his central character someone who is rejected by God and exiled from Heaven. The motive of forbidden love between mortals and gods also appeared in earlier works by Byron in *Heaven and Earth* (1821) and by Thomas Moore in *The Love of the Angels* (1823). The theme of breaking down the barriers between the celestial and human worlds and facing the consequences found permutations in Lermontov's poem. In Lermontov's *Demon* one can also see the echoes of a German romantic ballad, wherein a maiden has lost her fiancé before her wedding night, fused with ancient legends of the Caucasus about the beautiful Tamar, who was loved by a mountain spirit and died because of it. In Lermontov's poem the Demon is portrayed not as a force of evil but as a lonely romantic hero who is destined to eternal exile and unable to find the ideals of beauty and serenity toward which he is striving. The Russian artist Mikhail Vrubel illustrated the poem in 1891 and created a series of large paintings dedicated to Lermontov's *Demon*. They are currently at the Tretyakov Gallery in Moscow.

While in the Caucasus, Lermontov continued to write, and in 1840 he completed his famous novel *A Hero of Our Times*, in which he prophetically described a duel similar to the one in which he would lose his own life in 1841. *A Hero of Our Times* is considered the first Russian psychological novel. In it the narrative is arranged not in chronological order but as a gradual penetration into the internal world of the novel's main character, Pechorin. The Russian critic Vissarion Belinsky was the first to note this innovative structure. In his review in the influential literary magazine *Otechestvennye Zapiski* Belinsky wrote that Lermontov's novel contained a "deep knowledge of the human heart and of contemporary society" (глубо́кое зна́ние челове́ческого се́рдца и совреме́нного о́бщества). Belinsky highly praised the novel for its creation of a "completely new world of art" (соверше́нно но́вый мир иску́сства).

Pechorin shares many traits with a literary type that became known as a "Byronic hero": he exhibits great courage and passion, and at the same time he flaunts his boredom and distaste for society and social institutions, a position that leads him to rebellion or self-imposed exile; he is unfulfilled in love by social constraints or death; he possesses rank and privilege but has no respect for either; because of his arrogance and coldness he is unable to form lasting ties of either friendship or love.

When the novel first appeared, it was widely criticized because the critics thought that an immoral and callous person was made the central figure. The criticism prompted Lermontov to write a preface to a second edition in 1841, where he explained that the character of Pechorin was not his alter ego or a literary portrait of his friends but was instead a reflection of "the general vices of our society" (это портрет, составленный из пороков всего нашего поколения, в полном их развитии). Lermontov further said that for society the time had come for "bitter medicine and acid truth" (нужны горькие лекарства, едкие истины). The novel caused ardent literary polemics and has remained at the center of critical attention ever since.

Lermontov's life was tragically cut shot at the age of twenty-seven. On July 25, 1841, in Pyatigorsk one of his fellow officers, Nikolai Martynov, offended by Lermontov's jokes, challenged him to a duel. Friends of both Lermontov and Martynov hoped that the parties would make peace, and plans were even made for them to have dinner together later that evening. Everybody was so certain that the matter would be resolved amicably that a doctor was not called nor a carriage brought to the site of the duel in case one of the participants were wounded. As Lermontov started to raise his pistol, he was killed by Martynov's first shot. Lermontov was first buried at Pyatigorsk, but later his body was brought to the Tarkhany estate and buried alongside that of his mother.

Па́рус * (1832)

Беле́ет па́рус одино́кой	беле́ть – to show white; па́рус – sail; одино́кой – lonely
В **тума́не мо́ря** голубо́м! . .	тума́н –mist; мо́ре – sea
Что **и́щет** он в стране́ **далёкой**?	иска́ть – to look for; далёкий – distant
Что **ки́нул** он в **краю́ родно́м**? . . .	ки́нуть – *here:* to abandon; край родно́й – native land

Игра́ют **во́лны, ве́тер сви́щет,**	волна́ – wave; ве́тер – wind; свисте́ть – to whistle
И **ма́чта гнётся** и **скрыпи́т** . . .	ма́чта – mast; гну́ться – to bend; скрыпе́ть – to creak
Увы́! Он сча́стия не и́щет	увы́ – alas
И не от сча́стия бежи́т!	

Под ним **струя́ светле́й лазу́ри,**	струя́ – stream; све́тлый – light; лазу́рь *(f.)* – azure
Над ним **луч** со́лнца **золото́й** . . .	луч – ray; золото́й – golden
А он, **мятёжный, про́сит бу́ри,**	мятёжный – rebellious; проси́ть – to ask; бу́ря – storm
Как бу́дто в бу́рях есть **поко́й!**	как бу́дто – as if; поко́й – calm

Лексика и грамматика

1. Find all the examples of the Prepositional case (4). _____

_____

2. Find all the examples of the Instrumental case (2) and indicate the governing prepositions.

_____

3. "Одино́кий" means "lonely." Find the root and write down its meaning in English.

_____

What else can be described as одино́кий? Give your own examples.

_____

4. Write down all the color epithets that appear in the poem.

_____

_____

Make up your own sentences using these words _____

_____

Вопросы для обсуждения

1. What images and themes are mentioned in the poem? What does the poem evoke for you?

2. In thinking about Lermontov's biography, can you point to any events that could have contributed to the writing of this poem?

3. Write your own interpretation of the poem's main theme.

_____

_____

_____

_____

Расста́лись мы, но твой портре́т . . . * (1837)

This poem is dedicated to Varvara Lopukhina, whom Lermontov loved deeply all his life. Lermontov alludes to the last lines of the forty-two-volume autobiography of François-René de Chateaubriand, *Memoirs from beyond the Grave:* "God did not disappear, although his temple is deserted." It is important to mention that for Chateaubriand, who was a devout Catholic, these lines allude to divine love, while Lermontov reinterprets them to refer to his earthly love for a woman.

Расста́лись мы, но твой портре́т   расста́ться (с кем) – to part

Я на **груди́** мое́й **храню́**:   грудь *(f.)* – chest; храни́ть – to keep

Как **бле́дный при́зрак** лу́чших лет,   бле́дный – pale; при́зрак – ghost

Он **ду́шу ра́дует** мою́.   душа́ – soul; ра́довать – to bring joy to

И, но́вым **пре́данный страстя́м**,   пре́данный – given; страсть – passion

Я **разлюби́ть** его́ не мог: разлюби́ть – to stop loving

Так **храм оста́вленный – всё храм**,   храм – temple; оста́вленный – abandoned; всё – still

Куми́р пове́рженный – всё Бог!   куми́р – idol; пове́рженный – overthrown; Бог – God

Лексика и грамматика

1. Indicate the root and the prefixes in the verbs "влюби́ться" и "разлюби́ть."_____

_____. List any other words with the same root. _____

_____

2. Find the root in "пре́данный." _____. List other words with the same root.

_____

3. In the first line what case is used for "твой портре́т"?_____

4. In the second line of the second stanza, to what does "его́" refer?_____

Вопросы для обсуждения

1. What is the mood of the poem?

2. What are the main emotions in the poem?

3. What is the link between love and memory?

4. What does the poet imply about the nature of love? Does it ever disappear?

Моли́тва * (1839)

According to the memoirs of Alexandra Smirnova-Rossett (see below), Lermontov wrote this poem as a response to a suggestion by Maria Sherbatova with whom he was in love at that time to pray during moments of sadness. Another impetus for this poem may have come from Lermontov's friend Alexander Odoevsky, who in 1839 gave Lermontov the Gospels and the book *Добротолю́бие* (a collection of ancient Christian texts), translated by the archimandrite and Eastern Orthodox theologian Paisii Velichkovsky (1722–1794), who was later proclaimed a saint. Accompanying his gift, Odoevsky wrote a note to Lermontov in which he advised Lermontov to read the Gospels.

В мину́ту жи́зни тру́дную,

Тесни́тся ль в **се́рдце** грусть, тесни́ться *(Impf.)* – to press; се́рдце – heart

Одну́ **моли́тву чу́дную** моли́тва – prayer; чу́дный – miraculous

Твержу́ я наизу́сть. тверди́ть *(Impf.)* – to repeat; наизу́сть – by heart

Есть **си́ла благода́тная** си́ла – force; благода́тный – blessed

В **созву́чье** слов живы́х, созву́чье – harmony

И **ды́шит** непоня́тная, дыша́ть *(Impf.)* – to breathe

Свята́я пре́лесть в них. свято́й – sacred; пре́лесть *(f.)* – charm

С души́ как **бре́мя ска́тится,** бре́мя – burden; скати́ться *(Perf.)* – to roll off

Сомне́нье далеко́ – сомне́нье – doubt

И ве́рится, и пла́чется,

ве́рится – *cf.* ве́рить – to believe; пла́чется *cf.* пла́кать – to cry

И так легко́, легко́ . . .

легко́ – light

Лексика и грамматика

1. Find the prefix and the root in "созву́чие." _____

Write down their meanings in English._____

2. Find the prefix and the root in "непоня́тный."_____

Finish the following sentence: Мне непоня́тно_____

_____

3. In the last two lines of the poem, "И ве́рится, и пла́чется / И так легко́, легко́ . . .," the implied subject (мне) is ommitted. It is an example of the Dative subjectless construction describing an emotional or physical state (мне легко́, мне тру́дно, мне интере́сно, мне хо́чется, etc.) Make up two sentences using this construction.

_____

_____

Вопросы для обсуждения

1. What is the poem about?

2. How does the poet describe the beneficial effects of a prayer? Give specific examples from the text.

Из Гёте (Го́рные верши́ны . . .) * (1840)

This is Lermontov's free translation of a well-known poem by Goethe, "Wanderers Nachtlied II" ("Über allen Gipfeln . . ."), written in 1780. Goethe wrote this poem on an evening walk in the picturesque woods of Weimar, where he served at the court of the young duke Karl August. The poem was subsequently translated into Russian by several poets, including Innokenty Annensky, Valery Brusov, and Boris Pasternak. Lermontov's version is the most well known, and it was set to music by Alexander Varlamov.

Го́рные верши́ны	го́рный – mountain; верши́на – peak
Спят во **тьме** ночно́й;	тьма – darkness
Ти́хие доли́ны	ти́хий – quiet; доли́на – valley
По́лны све́жей мглой;	по́лный – full of; све́жий – fresh; мгла – mist, fog
Не **пыли́т доро́га,**	пыли́ть *(Impf.)* – to raise dust; доро́га – road
Не **дрожа́т листы́** . . .	дрожа́ть – to tremble; лист – leaf
Подожди́ немно́го,	
Отдохнёшь и ты.	

Ле́ксика и грамматика

1. "Ночно́й" and "ночь" share a common root. Can you find another adjective in the poem that

is also derived from a noun? _____

2. "Верши́на" means peak. The adjective "ве́рхний" means top. What is the common root?

_____

3. List all the nouns in the plural (3). _____

4. The verb "дрожа́ть" and the noun "дрожь" *(f.)* share a common root. Can you think of any

other examples with this verb? List them here. _____

_____

5. Find an example of the Imperative mood. _____

Вопросы для обсуждения

1. What is the atmosphere of the poem? What does the poem evoke for you?

2. Can you draw the night landscape that the poet describes?

3. How do you understand the last lines, "Подожди немного / Отдохнёшь и ты"?

Утёс * (1841)

Ночева́ла ту́чка золота́я	ночева́ть – to spend the night; ту́чка – cloud; золото́й – golden
На груди́ утёса – велика́на;	грудь *(f.)* – chest; утёс – rock; велика́н – giant
У́тром в путь она **умча́лась ра́но,**	умча́ться – to dash off; ра́но – early
По **лазу́ри** ве́село игра́я;	лазу́рь – azure
Но оста́лся **вла́жный след в морщи́не**	вла́жный – wet; след – trace; морщи́на – wrinkle
Ста́рого утёса. **Одино́ко**	одино́ко – lonely
Он стои́т, **заду́мался глубо́ко,**	заду́маться глубо́ко – to fall deep in thought
И **тихо́нько пла́чет** он в **пусты́не.**	тихо́нько – quietly; пла́кать – to cry; пусты́ня – *here:* wilderness

Лексика и грамматика

1. Find the root in "ночева́ть" and write down its meaning in English. _____

Make up a sentence with this verb._____

2. Find the root in "заду́маться." _____. List any words that share the same root.

_____

3. Find all the examples of the Prepositional case (3). _____

_____

4. List all the adverbs in the poem (5). _____

_____

Make up two sentences with these adverbs. _____

_____

Вопросы для обсуждения

1. In your opinion, what is the poem about?

2. What does the imagery of the poem suggest to you?

3. How does the poet convey the sadness of solitude? Find specific examples in the text.

А. О. Смирно́вой ** (1837)

This poem is dedicated to one of the most beautiful and intelligent women of St. Petersburg high society, Alexandra Smirnova-Rosset. Alexandra was a highly educated woman who frequented the literary circles of St. Petersburg and became a close friend of Pushkin, Vyazemsky, Lermontov, and Gogol. Pushkin and Vyazemsky also dedicated poems to her. She later wrote her memoirs, in which she described nineteenth-century life in St. Petersburg.

Без вас хочу́ сказа́ть вам мно́го,	без (+ *Gen.*) – without
При вас я слу́шать вас хочу́;	при вас – in your presence
Но **мо́лча** вы **гляди́те стро́го**,	мо́лча – silently; гляде́ть – to look; стро́го – stern
И я в **смуще́нии** молчу́.	смуще́ние – embarrassment

54

Что ж де́лать? **Ре́чью неиску́сной**   ре́чь *(f.)* – speech; неиску́сный – artless

Заня́ть ваш ум мне не дано́ . . .   заня́ть – to occupy; ум – mind; не дано́ *(idiom.)* – not for me

Всё это бы́ло бы **смешно́,**   смешно́ – funny

Когда́ бы не́ было так гру́стно.   Were it not so sad

Лексика и грамматика

1. Write down all the personal pronouns in the poem and indicate the case used in each

instance._____

_____

2. The preposition "без" means "without" and requires the Genitive case. The preposition "при" here means "in the presence of" and is followed by the Prepositional case. Be a poet and write a sentence with "при" and "без."

_____

_____

3. Заня́ть – заня́тия – за́нятый share a common root. Find the root and write down its meaning

in English. _____. Make up two sentences with these words.

_____

_____

4. Find an example of the subjunctive mood._____

Вопросы для обсуждения

1. What are the main emotions in the poem?

2. What are the poet's feelings toward the woman? Is he able to express them? Why not?

3. What can we say about their relationship?

У́зник ** (1837)

Lermontov wrote this poem while he was under arrest awaiting trial for his poem "Death of a Poet." He was twenty-three years old, the same age as Pushkin had been when he wrote his poem bearing the same title (see above).

Отвори́те мне **темни́цу,**	отвори́ть *(Perf.)* – to open; темни́ца – prison
Да́йте мне **сия́нье** дня,	сия́нье – radiance
Черногла́зую деви́цу,	черногла́зый – black-eyed; деви́ца – maiden
Черногри́вого коня́.	черногри́вый – black-maned; конь – horse
Я краса́вицу **младу́ю**	младо́й *(poet.)* – young
Пре́жде сла́дко **поцелу́ю,**	пре́жде – *here:* first; поцелова́ть *(Perf.)* – to kiss
На коня́ пото́м **вскочу́,**	вскочи́ть *(Perf.)* – to jump on
В **степь,** как **ве́тер,** улечу́.	степь *(f.)* – steppe; ве́тер – wind

Но окно́ **тюрьмы́ высо́ко,**	тюрьма́ – prison; высо́кий – high
Дверь **тяжёлая** с **замко́м;**	тяжёлый – heavy; зам/о́/к – lock
Черноо́кая далёко,	черноо́кий *(poet.)* – черногла́зый; далёкий – far
В **пы́шном те́реме** своём;	пы́шный – sumptuous; те́рем *(arch.)* – Russian wooden palace

До́брый конь в зелёном **по́ле**	по́ле – field
Без **узды́**, оди́н, по **во́ле**	узда́ – bridle; во́ля – freedom
Ска́чет ве́сел и игри́в,	скака́ть *(Impf.)* – to gallop; ве́сел – cheerful; игри́в – playful
Хвост по ве́тру **распусти́в.**	хвост – tail; распусти́ть *(Perf.)* – *here:* to spread

Одино́к я – нет отра́ды:	одино́к – lonely; отра́да *(poet.)* – joy
Сте́ны го́лые круго́м,	стена́ – wall; го́лый – *here:* bare
Ту́скло све́тит **луч лампа́ды**	ту́склый – dim; луч – ray; лампа́да *(arch.)* – lamp
Умира́ющим огнём;	умира́ющий – dying; ого́нь – fire

То́лько слы́шно: за дверя́ми	
Зву́чно – ме́рными шага́ми	зву́чный – resonant; ме́рный – meausured; шаг – step
Хо́дит в **тишине́** ночно́й	тишина́ – silence; stillness
Безотве́тный часово́й.	безотве́тный – nonresponsive; часово́й – sentinel

Лексика и грамматика

1. Find the roots in черногла́зый – черноо́кий – черногри́вый. Write down its meaning in

English. _____ . What does

"черноволо́сый" mean? _____ . Make up two sentences with these words.

_____

_____

2. Find the prefix and the root in "безотве́тный" and write down their meanings in English.

_____

Can you think of any analogous adjectives? (If you need help, see Pushkin's "Я вас

люби́л. . . .") Make up a sentence with this word._____

_____

3. Find all the imperatives in the poem. What is their aspect?_____

_____

4. Be a poet and finish the following sentence: Да́йте мне_____

_____!

Вопро́сы для обсужде́ния

1. What is the poem about?

2. How does the mood of the poem change from the first to the second to the third stanza?

3. Compare this poem with Pushkin's poem with the same title.

И ску́чно, и гру́стно . . . ** (1840)

И ску́чно и гру́стно, и не́кому ру́ку пода́ть	there is no one to whom I can reach out my hand
В мину́ту душе́вной невзго́ды . . .	душе́вный – *cf.* душа́ – soul; невзго́да – adversity
Жела́нья! . . . что по́льзы напра́сно и ве́чно жела́ть? . . .	жела́нье – desire; по́льза – use;
напра́сно	– in vain; ве́чно – eternally

А го́ды **прохо́дят** – все лу́чшие го́ды!   проходи́ть – to pass

Люби́ть . . . но кого́ же? . . . **на вре́мя – не сто́ит труда́,** – temporarily – it is not worth the effort

А **ве́чно** люби́ть **невозмо́жно.**   ве́чно – eternally, forever; невозмо́жно –

          impossible

В себя́ ли **загля́нешь**? – там про́шлого нет и **следа́:** загляну́ть *(Perf.)* – to look into; след – trace

И ра́дость, и **му́ки,** и всё там **ничто́жно** . . .   му́ка – torment; ничто́жно – insignificant

Что **стра́сти**? – ведь ра́но иль по́здно их сла́дкий **неду́г** стра́сть *(f.)* – passion; ведь – *here:* you

          know; неду́г – affliction

Исче́знет при сло́ве **рассу́дка;**   исче́знуть – to disappear; при – *here:* at; рассу́д/о/к

          – reason

И жизнь, как посмо́тришь с холо́дным **внима́ньем** вокру́г –   внима́нье – attention

Така́я **пуста́я** и глу́пая **шу́тка** . . .   пусто́й – empty; шу́тка – joke

Ле́ксика и грамма́тика

1. Жела́нье –жела́ть (+ *Gen.*) – жела́нный share a common root. Find the root and write down

its meaning in English. _____. Make up two sentences using any of these words.

_____

_____

2. Заглянуть (в/на + Acc.) – гляде́ть (в/на + *Acc.*) – взгляд share a common root. Find the root and write down its meaning in English. _____. Make up two sentences using any of these words. _____

_____

3. Проходи́ть – про́шлое share a common prefix and root. Find the prefix and the root and write down their meanings in English. Make up two sentences with these words.

_____

_____

4. List all the infinitives in the poem (3). _____

_____

5. Find some examples of subjectless sentences._____

_____

_____

Вопросы для обсуждения

1. What is the mood of the poem?

2. What are the oppositions set up in the poem?

3. What is the poet's view of love, desire, and passion? Do you agree or disagree with his assessment? Explain your point of view.

Ту́чи ** (1840)

According to the recollections of Count Vladimir Sollogub, this poem was written on the eve of Lermontov's departure from St. Petersburg to his exile in the Caucasus. Friends of the poet gathered at the apartment of a prominent Russian author and historian, Nikolai Karamzin, whose widow, Yekaterina, and daughter, Sophia, held a literary salon for a farewell party for Lermontov. The poet looked out the window at the clouds above the Neva River and recited this poem. When Lermontov finished reciting it, his friends had tears in their eyes.

Ту́чки небе́сные, **ве́чные стра́нники**!	ту́чка – cloud; ве́чный – eternal; стра́нник – wanderer
Сте́пью лазу́рною, це́пью жемчу́жною	степь *(f.)* – steppe; лазу́рный – azure; цепь *(f.)* – chain; жемчу́жный – pearly
Мчи́тесь вы, **бу́дто** как я же, **изгна́нники**	мча́ться – to rush; бу́дто – as if; изгна́нник – exile
С ми́лого **се́вера** в **сто́рону ю́жную**.	се́вер – north; сторона́ – side; *here:* region; ю́жный – southern
Кто же вас **го́нит: судьбы́** ли реше́ние?	гнать – to chase; судьба́ – fate
За́висть ли **та́йная**? **Зло́ба** ль откры́тая?	за́висть *(f.)* – envy; та́йный – secret; зло́ба – malice
Или на вас **тяготи́т преступле́ние**?	тяготи́ть – to weigh heavily; преступле́ние – crime
Или друзе́й **клевета́ ядови́тая**?	клевета́ – slander; ядови́тый – poisonous
Нет, вам **наску́чили ни́вы беспло́дные** . . .	наску́чить – to bore; ни́ва *(poet.)* – field; беспло́дный – barren
Чу́жды вам **стра́сти** и чу́жды **страда́ния**;	чу́ждый – alien; страсть – passion; страда́ние – suffering
Ве́чно холо́дные, ве́чно **свобо́дные**,	ве́чно – eternally; свобо́дный – free
Нет у вас **ро́дины**, нет вам **изгна́ния**.	ро́дина – motherland; изгна́ние – exile

Ле́ксика и грамма́тика

1. Find the common root in изгна́ние – изгна́нник – гнать and write down its meaning in English. _____

2. Find the common root in зло́ба – злой and write down its meaning in English.

_____

3. "Тяготи́ть" means "to weigh heavily." An adjective with the same root also exists: "тяжёлый."

Find the common root and write down its meaning in English._____

What can be described as "тяжёлый"? Make up two sentences with these words._____

_____

_____

4. Find all the third-declension nouns (4) and list them here. _____

_____

Вопросы для обсуждения

1. What are the images and themes mentioned in the poem?

2. Using Internet resources, find what specific events in Lermontov's life contributed to the writing of this poem.

3. What are the main oppositions set up in the poem?

4. What does the poem evoke for you?

Сосна́ ** (1841)

Like "Го́рные верши́ны," this poem was also written as a free translation of a German poem, "Ein Fichtenbaum steht einsam," by Heinrich Heine. In Heine's poem a pine tree is dreaming about a beautiful sad palm. Lermontov used the same imagery to convey the themes of loneliness and unfulfilled love. Heine's poem was translated many times by other Russian poets, including Fyodor Tyutchev, Afanasy Fet, and Zinaida Gippius.

На **се́вере ди́ком** стои́т **одино́ко**   се́вер – north; ди́кий – wild; одино́ко – lonely

На **го́лой верши́не сосна́**   го́лый – bare; верши́на – peak; сосна́ – pine

И **дре́млет, кача́ясь,** и сне́гом **сыпу́чим**   дрема́ть – to doze; кача́ясь – swaying; сыпу́чий – loose

Оде́та, как **ри́зой**, она́.   оде́т – dressed; ри́за – chasuble

И **сни́тся** ей всё, что в **пусты́не далёкой,**   сни́ться (кому) – to dream; пусты́ня – desert; далёкий –

distant

В том **кра́е**, где **со́лнца восхо́д,**   кра́й – *here:* land; со́лнце – sun; восхо́д – sunrise

Одна́ и грустна́ на **утёсе горю́чем**   утёс – rock; горю́чий *(poet.)* – hot

Прекра́сная па́льма растёт.   прекра́сный – beautiful; па́льма – palm; расти́ – to grow

Лексика и грамматика

1. Find the root in "прекра́сный" and write down its meaning in English._____

_____ . List any other words with the same root here._____

_____

What else can be described as "прекра́сный"? Give your own examples._____

_____

2. Find the prefix and the root in "восхо́д" and write down their meanings in

English._____

3. "Одино́кий" and "оди́н" share a common root. Find the root and write down its meaning in

English. _____

Who or what can be described as "одино́кий"? Make up two sentences with this word.

_____

4. Find all the adjectives in the poem (8) and list them here. _____

_____

Вопросы для обсуждения

1. What are the images mentioned in the poem?

2. What are the main oppositions set up in the poem?

3. In your opinion, what is the poem about? How does this poem compare to "Утёс"?

4. What is the overall mood of the poem?

Сон ** (1841)

In the eighteenth century, Peter the Great annexed Dagestan as a result of the first Russo-Persian War, but over the course of history there have been many battles between imperial Russia and the mountain insurgents supporting Islam. The poem alludes to the Caucasian War of 1817–1864, going on at the time of Lermontov's service in the Caucasus; the confrontations there were especially intense.

В **полдне́вный жар** в **доли́не Дагеста́на**	полдне́вный – midday; жар – heat; доли́на – valley; Дагеста́н – territory located in the North Causasus, bordered by the Caspian Sea
С **свинцо́м** в **груди́** лежа́л **недви́жим** я;	свин/е́/ц – lead; грудь (f.) – chest; недви́жим – motionless
Глубо́кая ещё **дыми́лась ра́на,**	глубо́кий – deep; дыми́ться (Impf.) – to smoke; ра́на – wound
По **ка́пле кровь точи́лася** моя́.	ка́пля – drop; кровь (f.) – blood; точи́ться (Impf.) – here: to ooze

Лежа́л оди́н я на **песке́** доли́ны;   пес/о́/к – sand

Усту́пы скал тесни́лися круго́м,   усту́п – ledge; скала́ – rock; тесни́ться *(Impf.)* – to cluster;

                                                         круго́м – around

И со́лнце **жгло** их жёлтые **верши́ны**   жечь *(Impf.)* – to burn; верши́на – peak

И жгло меня́ – но спал **я мёртвым** сном.   мёртвый – dead

И сни́лся мне **сия́ющий огня́ми**   сия́ющий – radiant; ог/о́/нь – *here:* light

Вече́рний **пир в роди́мой стороне́.**   пир – feast; роди́мый – native; сторона́ – *here:* land

Меж ю́ных **жён, увéнчанных** цвета́ми,   меж *(arch.)* – между – among; жена́ *(arch.)* – *here:* woman;

                                                         увéнчанный – crowned

Шёл разгово́р весёлый обо мне.

Но в разгово́р весёлый **не вступа́я,**   не вступа́я – not joining

Сиде́ла там **заду́мчиво** одна́,   заду́мчиво – pensively

И в гру́стный сон душа́ её **млада́я**   млада́й *(poet.)* – молодо́й – young

Бог зна́ет чем была́ **погружена́;**   Бог зна́ет чем – God knows by what; погружена́ – immersed

И сни́лась ей доли́на Дагеста́на;

Знако́мый **труп** лежа́л в доли́не той;   труп – corpse

В его груди́ **дымя́сь** черне́ла ра́на,   дымя́сь – steaming

И кровь **лила́сь хладе́ющей струёй**   ли́ться *(Impf.)* – *here:* to flow; хладе́ющий –

                                                         cooling; струя́ – stream

Лексика и грамматика

1. Сон – сни́ться (+Dative) – присни́ться (+ *D*.) share a common root. Find the root and write down its meaning and the meaning of the words in English._____

Be a poet and finish the following sentence: Мне сни́лось, _____

2. "Чёрный" means "black." What does "чернéть" mean?_____

3. Find all the participles in the poem (5), write down their meaning in English, and write down the infinitives of these verbs. _____

_____

4. Find the gerunds in the poem (2) and write down the infinitives of these verbs. _____

_____

Make up a sentence with one of the gerunds._____

_____

Вопросы для обсуждения

1. What happens in the poem?

2. How many dreams are in the poem? What is the dream of the lyric hero?

3. What is the dream of the young woman?

4. Vladimir Solovyev, a Russian philosopher and poet of the Silver Age, called this poem "Сон в ку́бе" – "a dream to the third power." How do you understand his words?

Выхожу́ оди́н я на доро́гу . . . ** (1841)

This is one of Lermontov's last poems. It is thought that the images in it evoke a celebrated poem by Henrich Heine, "Der Tod, das ist die kühle Nacht ..." from his collection *Buch der Lieder* (1827), which Lermontov read and admired. The image of a tree is present also in Heine's poem, and the image of an oak seen by Prince Andrey after he meets Natasha later appeared in Tolstoy's *War and Peace* as a symbol of spiritual rebirth.

Выхожу́ оди́н я на **доро́гу**;	доро́га – road
Сквозь **тума́н кремни́стый** путь **блести́т**;	тума́н – mist; кремни́стый – stony; блесте́ть – to shine
Ночь тиха́. **Пусты́ня вне́млет Бо́гу**,	пусты́ня – desert; внемле́ть *(arch.)* – to listen to; Бо́г – God
И **звезда́** с звездо́ю говори́т.	звезда́ – star
В **небеса́х торже́ственно и чу́дно**!	небеса́ – sky, heavens; торже́ственно – solemn; чу́дно – wondrous
Спит земля́ в **сия́нье голубо́м** . . .	земля́ – earth; сия́нье – radiance; голубо́й – light blue
Что же мне так бо́льно и так тру́дно?	
Жду **ль** чего́? **жале́ю** ли о чём?	ль – ли – *here:* question particle; жале́ть – to regret
Уж не жду от жи́зни ничего́ я,	уж не – уже́ не – no longer
И не **жаль** мне **про́шлого ничу́ть**;	жаль – to regret; про́шлое – past; ничу́ть – not at all
Я **ищу́ свобо́ды и поко́я**!	иска́ть – to look for; свобо́да – freedom; поко́й – calm
Я б хотел **забы́ться и засну́ть**!	б – бы – would; забы́ться – to become oblivious; засну́ть – to fall asleep

Но не тем холодным **сном могилы** . . .	сон – sleep; могила – grave
Я б **желал навеки** так заснуть,	желать – to wish; навеки – forever
Чтоб в **груди дремали** жизни **силы**,	чтоб – чтобы – in order to; грудь – chest; дремать – to doze; сила – force
Чтоб, **дыша, вздымалась** тихо грудь;	дыша – breathing; вздыматься – to heave
Чтоб всю ночь, весь день мой **слух лелея**,	слух – ear; лелеять – *here:* to caress
Про любовь мне **сладкий голос** пел,	сладкий – sweet; голос – voice
Надо мной чтоб, **вечно зеленея**,	вечно – eternally; зеленея – staying green
Тёмный дуб склонялся и шумел.	тёмный – dark; дуб – oak; склоняться – to lean; шуметь – to rustle

Лексика и грамматика

1. Find the gerunds in the poem (3) and write down the infinitives of these verbs. _____

_____

2. Find all the examples of the Conditional mood and provide the English translations. _____

_____

3. Be a poet and finish the following sentence: Я б хотел/а _____

4. List all the adverbs in the poem. _____

_____

Make up two sentences with these adverbs.

_____

_____

Вопросы для обсуждения

1. What is the mood of the poem?

2. What are the poem's main themes?

3. What is the poet's attitude toward the beauty of nature?

4. What can be inferred about the span of human life vs. nature? How does the poem illustrate it?

5. What does the imagery of the poem evoke for you?

Евге́ний Абра́мович Барать́нский (1800–1844)

Yevgeny Baratynsky (also spelled Boratynsky) belongs to the circle of Russian poets who were among Pushkin's friends and contemporaries. This period, which had its peak during the 1820s and early 1830s, would later become known as the "Золото́й век ру́сской поэзии"—the Golden Age of Russian poetry—because of the richeness of the poetic legacy that it has produced. Baratynsky was a master of the small forms of lyric poetry, notably the elegy. "Baratynsky is a charm and a miracle. After him I will never again publish my elegies," wrote Pushkin to another writer, Alexander Bestuzhev-Marlinsky. Baratynsky's central themes are love, introspection, and the relationship among man, nature and the universe. Dmitry Mirsky in his *History of Russian Literature* (p. 103) described Baratynsky as someone who strove for a fuller union with nature, and this aspiration for a more organic and natural existence was one of the main motives of his poetry. During his short life Baratynsky published several books of poems, but despite the great esteem of some poets and critics, the general public received them coldly. When Baratynsky died after a sudden illness during a journey to Italy in 1844, he was already almost forgotten by his

contemporaries, but his poems were rediscovered at the end of the nineteenth century by the

Russian Symbolist poets.

Уверéние ** (1824)

Нет, обманýла вас молвá,	обманýть – to deceive; молвá – talk
По-прéжнему дышý я вáми,	по-прéжнему – still; дышáть – to breathe
И надо мной свой **правá**	правá – rights
Вы не **утрáтили с годáми.**	утрáтить – to lose; с годáми – *here:* over the years
Другúм **курúл я фимиáм,**	курúть фимиáм *(idiom.)* – to sing praises
Но вас носúл в **святы́не сéрдца**;	святы́ня – sanctuary; сéрдце – heart
Молúлся нóвым **образáм,**	молúться (кому) – to pray; образá – icons
Но с **беспокóйством старовéрца.**	беспокóйство – uneasiness; старовéр/е/ц – Old Believer

In 1653 Patriach Nikon instituted broad reforms within the Russian Orthodox Church dealing with changes in the ritual and making it consistent with the Greek Orthodox Church. These reforms led to the split in the Russian chuch that is known as *raskol*. Those who did not support the reforms of Patriach Nikon were referred to as старовéрцы or старовéры (Old Believers) or раскóльники (Splitters) or старообрядцы (*lit.* those following the old customs).

Лексика и грамматика

1. Find the prefix and the root in "беспокóйство" and write down their meanings in English.

_____

Can you think of any other words with the same root? _____

2. Find the roots in "старовéрец." and write down their meanings in English. _____

_____

72

List any other words consisting of two roots. _____

_____

3. Find all the uses of the pronoun "вы," and in each instance write down the case and the

governing verb. _____

_____

4. Find all the verbs in the past tense and analyze the aspectual choice. What is the aspect used in

the first part of the poem? _____

 What is the aspect used in the second part of the poem and why?_____

Вопросы для обсуждения

1. What is the tone of the poem?

2. Whom does the poet address?

3. Does the poet still love her? How do you know?

4. Compare this poem and Lermontov's "Расстались мы, но твой портрет . . ." above. Do you
see any similarities between the two poems? Are they similar to or different from Pushkin's "Я
вас любил . . ." above? Explain your point of view.

Где сла́дкий шёпот мои́х лесо́в? . . . ** (1831)

Где **сла́дкий шёпот**	сла́дкий – sweet; шёпот – whisper
Мои́х лесо́в?	
Пото́ков ро́пот,	пото́к – stream; ро́пот – murmur
Цветы́ **луго́в**?	луг – meadow
Дере́вья го́лы;	дере́вья – trees; го́лы – *cf.* го́лый – bare

Ковёр зимы́	ков/ё/р – carpet
Покры́л холмы́,	покры́ть – to cover; холм – hill
Луга́ и до́лы.	луг – meadow; дол *(poet.)* – dale, vale
Под **ледяно́й**	ледяно́й – icy
Свое́й **коро́й**	кора́ – crust
Ручей неме́ет;	ручей – brook; неме́ть *(Impf.)* – to grow mute
Всё **цепене́ет,**	цепене́ть *(Impf.)* – to freeze
Лишь ве́тер злой,	лишь – only
Бушу́я, во́ет	бушу́я – raging; выть *(Impf., во́ю, во́ешь)* – to howl
И не́бо **кро́ет**	крыть *(Impf., кро́ю, кро́ешь)* – to cover
Седо́ю мглой.	седо́й – gray (in reference to hair only); мгла – darkness

Лексика и грамматика

1. Кро́ет – покры́ть – покрыва́ло share a common root. Find the root and write down its

meaning in English. _____ . Make up a sentence with any of these words.

_____

2. Онеме́ть – немо́й – не́м/е/ц – неме́цкий share a common root. Find the root and write down

its meaning in English. _____ . Make up two sentences with any of these

words. _____

_____

3. List all the nouns in the plural (7).

_____

Make up three sentences with these words. _____

4. List all the verbs in the present tense (4). _____

_____. Make up a sentence with any

of these verbs. _____

Вопросы для обсуждения

1. What is the mood of the landscape?

2. Does the poet love winter?

3. How does this poem compare to Pushkin's "Зимнее у́тро" and "Зимний ве́чер" above?

Весна́, весна́! Как во́здух чист! . . . ** (1832)

Весна́, весна́! как **во́здух чист!**	во́здух – air; чист – *cf.* чи́стый – pure
Как **я́сен небосклóн!**	я́сен – *cf.* я́сный – clear; небосклóн – horizon
Своéй **лазу́рию живóй**	лазу́рь *(f.)* – azure; живóй – *here:* vivid
Слепи́т мне óчи он.	слепи́ть *(Impf.)* – to blind; óчи *(arch.)* – eyes
Весна́, весна́! как **высокó**	высокó – high
На **кры́льях ветеркá,**	кры́лья – wings; ветер/ó/к *(dim.)* – wind
Ласкáясь к **сóлнечным лучáм,**	ласкáясь – caressing; сóлнечные лучи́ – rays of the sun
Летáют **облакá!**	облакá – clouds

Шумя́т ручьи́! блестя́т ручьи́!	шуме́ть *(Impf.)* – *here:* to rustle; ручьи́ – springs; блесте́ть *(Impf.)* – to sparkle
Взреве́в, река́ несёт	взреве́в – roaring
На **торжеству́ющем хребте́**	торжеству́ющий – triumphant; хреб/е/т – *here:* back
Подня́тый ею лёд!	подня́тый – raised; л/ё/д – ice
Ещё **древа́ обнажены́,**	древа́ *(arch.)* – trees; обнажены́ – bare
Но в **ро́ще ве́тхий лист,**	ро́ща – grove; ве́тхий – decrepit; лист – leaf
Как пре́жде, под мое́й **ного́й**	как пре́жде – as before; нога́ – foot
И **шу́мен** и **души́ст.**	шу́мен – шу́мный – rustling; души́ст – души́стый – fragrant
Под со́лнце са́мое **взвился́**	взви́ться *(Perf.)* – to fly up
И в **я́ркой вышине́**	я́ркий – bright; вышина́ – height
Незри́мый жа́воронок поёт	незри́мый – invisible; жа́воронок – lark
Заздра́вный гимн весне́.	hymn to the health of spring
Что с не́ю, что с мое́й душо́й?	
С **ручьём** она́ ручей	ручей – spring
И с **пти́чкой** пти́чка! С ним **журчи́т,**	пти́чка *(dim.)* – bird; журча́ть *(Impf.)* – to babble
Лета́ет в не́бе с ней!	

Зачём так **ра́дует** её	ра́довать *(Impf.)* – to gladden, cheer
И со́лнце, и весна́!	
Лику́ет ли, как дочь **стихи́й,**	ликова́ть *(Impf.)* – jubilate; стихи́я – elements
На **пи́ре** их она́?	пир – feast

Что ну́жды! сча́стлив, кто на нём	что ну́жды – what is the need?
Забве́нье мы́сли пьёт,	забве́нье – oblivion; мысль *(f.)* – thought
Кого́ **далёко** от неё	далёко – far
Он, **ди́вный, унесёт!**	ди́вный – wondrous; унести́ *(Perf.)* – to carry away

Лексика и грамматика

1. Find the two roots in "небоскло́н" and write down their meanings in English. _____

_____

2. Ра́довать – рад – ра́дость share a common root. Find the root and write down its meaning in

English. _____. Make up two sentences with these words. _____

_____

3. Шуме́ть – шу́мный – шу́мен – шум share a common root. Find the root and write down its

meaning in English. _____ . Make up two sentences with these words.

_____

_____

4. "Забве́нье" is formed from the verb "забыва́ть." Find the root and write down its meaning in English. _____ . Make up a sentence with this verb._____

_____

5. In the fifth stanza, "Заче́м так ра́дует её / И со́лнце, и весна́! /Лику́ет ли, как дочь стихи́й / На пи́ре их она́?," to what does "она́" refer? What cases are used in each sentence?_____

_____

6. In the last stanza, "Сча́стлив, кто на нём / Забве́нье мы́сли пьёт, / Кого́ далёко от неё / Он, ди́вный, унесёт!," to what does "он" refer? What cases are used in each sentence?_____

_____

Вопросы для обсуждения

1. What is the mood of the poem?

2. How does the poet describe spring?

3. How does the poet's soul respond to the spring awakening of nature? Can you cite specific examples from the poem?

4. Compare this poem with Tyutchev's "Весе́нняя гроза́" and Fet's "Я пришёл к тебе́ с приве́том . . ." below.

Разуве́рение *** (1821)

Не **искуша́й** меня́ без **ну́жды**	искуша́ть – to tempt; ну́жда – need
Возвра́том не́жности твое́й:	возвра́т – return; не́жность *(f.)* – affection
Разочаро́ванному чу́жды	разочаро́ванный – disappointed; чу́жды – alien

78

Все **обольще́нья пре́жних** дней!	обольще́нье – enticement; пре́жний – *here:* old
Уж я не ве́рю **увере́ньям,**	увере́нье – assurance
Уж я не **ве́рую** в любо́вь,	ве́ровать *(Impf.)* – to believe
И не могу́ **преда́ться** вновь	преда́ться *(Perf.)* – to give oneself over to
Раз измени́вшим сновиде́ньям!	раз – once; измени́вший – betrayed; сновиде́нье – dream
Слепо́й тоски́ мое́й не **мно́жь,**	слепо́й – blind; тоска́ – longing; мно́жить – to multiply
Не **заводи́** о **пре́жнем** слова,	заводи́ть – *here:* to start; пре́жнее – past
И, друг **забо́тливый,** больно́го	забо́тливый – caring
В его **дремо́те** не **трево́жь!**	дремо́та – doze; трево́жить *(Impf.)* – to disturb
Я сплю, мне сла́дко **усыпле́нье;**	усыпле́нье *(arch.)* – sleep
Забу́дь **быва́лые мечты́:**	быва́лый – former; мечта́ – dream
В душе́ мое́й одно́ **волне́нье,**	волне́нье – agitation
А не любо́вь **пробу́дишь** ты.	пробуди́ть *(Perf.)* – to awaken

Лексика и грамматика

1. Разуве́ренье – ве́рить (+ *D.*) – ве́ровать *(relig.; в + Acc.)* – увере́нье share a common root.

Find the root and write down its meaning and the meaning of the words in English.

_____

_____

Make up two sentences using ве́рить и ве́ровать._____

_____

2. "Сновиде́нье" means "dream." Find the two roots and write down their meanings in English.

_____

3. Спать – усыпля́ть – усыпле́нье share a common root. Find the root and write down its meaning and the meaning of the words in English.

_____

4. Find all the imperatives in the poem (5). _____

_____

Вопросы для обсуждения

1. Why is the poem called "Разуве́ние"?

2. Whom is the lyrical poet addressing?

3. How did their relationship change?

4. What does he say about the nature of his feelings?

Фёдор Ива́нович Тю́тчев (1803–1873)

Fyodor Tyutchev, along with Pushkin and Lermontov, is acknowledged to be one of the three greatest Russian poets of the nineteenth century. A profesional diplomat and prominent statesman, over the course of his life Fyodor Tyutchev wrote about three hundred short lyrical poems, of which few were published in his lifetime. However, his poetic legacy was so remarkable that Lev Tolstoy considered him his favorite poet, along with Pushkin, saying that Tyutchev was "deeper than Pushkin."

Tyutchev was born into a noble family in Ovstug, near Bryansk, in southwestern Russia. His literary talents and brilliant mind were evident early on; at the age of twelve he had already translated Horace. First educated at home, later Tyutchev studied in the Department of History and Philology at Moscow University.

After graduation he joined the Foreign Office and, thanks to the efforts of his uncle, was given a post at the Russian diplomatic mission in Munich, where he remained for over twenty years. Both of Tyutchev's wives were German. He married a young widow, Eleonore von Bothmer, who died in 1838, and then married Ernestine von Dernberg, who followed him to Russia in 1844. Neither of the wives spoke Russian, but Ernestine made an effort to learn the language later in life. There was a voluminous correspondence between Tyutchev and Ernestine in French, but Ernestine later destroyed most of their early letters. It is thought that Tyutchev's poem "Она сидела на полу . . . ," included in this book, was written to Ernestine and reflects this part of his personal life.

After his return to Russia, Tyutchev played an important role in Russia's foreign policy as a chief adviser to Russia's foreign minister, Mikhail Gorchakov. Tyutchev was also the chairman of the Committee of Foreign Censorship. His political views were quite conservative. He supported the monarchy, and as a censor, he banned the translation into Russian of Karl Marx's *Capital,* saying, "Those who are interested can read it in German." He was close to the Slavophiles and believed in a unique Russian national identity. Tyutchev had a prominent political career and eventually received the title of privy councillor, the second-highest ranking in the *Table of Ranks* of imperial Russia.

In the last years of his life Tyutchev suffered many personal losses. His last love and common-law wife, Yelena Denisyeva (see note below), with whom he had three children in the fifteen years they were together, died at the age of thirty-six from tuberculousis, and so did two of their children. Tyutchev's eldest son Dmitry and daughter Maria (from his second marriage) also died, as did his brother Nikolai. These tragic events plunged Tyutchev into a depression. He suffered a series of strokes and died in 1873.

Зима́ неда́ром зли́тся . . . ** (1830)

Зима́ **неда́ром зли́тся,**	неда́ром – not without reason; зли́ться *(Impf.)* – to be angry
Прошла́ её **пора́** –	пора́ – *here:* time
Весна́ в окно́ **стучи́тся**	стуча́ться *(Impf.)* – to knock
И **го́нит со двора́.**	гнать со двора́ *(idiom.)* – to send on one's way
И всё **засуети́лось,**	засуети́ться *(Perf., colloq.)* – to scurry
Всё **ну́дит** Зи́му **вон** –	нуди́ть *(arch., Impf.)* – to force; вон – out
И **жа́воронки** в не́бе	жа́ворон/о/к – lark
Уж **по́дняли трезво́н.**	уж – уже́ – already; подня́ть трезво́н *(idiom.)* – to raise a clamor
Зима́ ещё **хлопо́чет**	хлопота́ть *(Impf.)* – to hustle about
И на Весну́ **ворчи́т:**	ворча́ть *(Impf., colloq.)* – to grumble
Та ей **в глаза́ хохо́чет**	хохота́ть в глаза́ *(idiom., Impf.)* – to laugh in one's face
И **пу́ще лишь шуми́т . . .**	пу́ще *(colloq.)* – more; лишь – only; шуме́ть *(Impf.)* – to make noise
Взбеси́лась ве́дьма зла́я	взбеси́ться *(colloq., Perf.)* – to lash out; ве́дьма – witch

И, снéгу **захватя́**,	снéг – snow; захватя́ – having grabbed
Пусти́ла, убегáя,	пусти́ть *(Perf.)* – to launch
В прекрáсное **дитя́** . . .	дитя́ *(poet.)* – child

Веснé и **гóря мáло**:	гóря мáло (+ *D.; colloq.*) – [she/he] does not care a bit
Умы́лася в снегý	умы́ться *(Perf.)* – to wash one's face
И лишь **румя́ней** стáла	румя́ней – rosier (in reference to cheeks)
Наперекóр врагý.	наперекóр (+ *D.*)– *here:* in defiance; враг – enemy

Лексика и грамматика

1. Зли́ться – злой – зло share a common root. Find the root and write down its meaning in

English. _____. Make up a sentence with any of these words.

_____

2. Дитя́ – дéтский – дéтство share a common root. Find the root and write down its meaning in

English. _____ . Make up two sentences with these words.

_____

_____

3. List three things that winter and spring do in the poem: Зимá _____,

_____, а веснá _____

4. List two Imperfective gerunds and the verbs from which they are formed. Write down their

meanings in English._____

5. Find all the reflexive verbs in the poem (5)._____

_____

Make up two sentences with any of these verbs. _____

_____

Вопросы для обсуждения

1. What is the poem about? In your opinion, what month of the year is the poet describing?

2. How are winter and spring portrayed?

3. How is the battle between reluctant, grouchy winter and young, triumphant spring described?

4. What does the poem evoke for you?

Весéнние вóды ** (1829)

This poem describes spring in Bavaria, where Tyutchev was living at the time he wrote it.

Ещё в **полях** белéет снег,	пóле – field
А вóды уж весной шумя́т –	but the waters are already burbling with the sounds of spring
Бегу́т и **бу́дят сóнный брег,**	буди́ть *(Impf.)* – to awaken; сóнный – sleepy; брег *(arch.)* – bank
Бегу́т, и **блéщут, и глася́т** . . .	блестéть *(Impf.)* – to glisten; гласи́ть *(Impf.)* – to announce
Они́ глася́т **во все концы́:**	во все концы́ – in every direction
"**Весна́** идёт, весна́ идёт,	весна́ идёт – spring is coming
Мы молодóй весны́ **гонцы́,**	гон/é/ц – messenger
Она́ нас вы́слала вперёд!"	She sent us ahead

86

Весна́ идёт, весна́ идёт,

И **ти́хих, тёплых** ма́йских дней   ти́хий – quiet; тёплый – warm

Румя́ный, све́тлый хорово́д   румя́ный – rosy; све́тлый – light; хорово́д – reel

Толпи́тся ве́село за не́й! . . .   толпи́ться *(Impf.)* – to crowd

Лексика и грамматика

1. "Май" means "May." What does "ма́йский" mean?_____

Make up a sentence with these words.

_____

2. Сон – со́нный – сни́ться (+ *D.*) share a common root. Find the root and write down its

meaning in English. _____. Make up a sentence with any of these words.

_____

3. Гласи́ть – го́лос – голосова́ть share a common root. Find the root and write down its

meaning in English. _____. Make up a sentence with any of these words.

_____

4. List all the verbs (5) describing what the spring waters are doing. Hint: look for verbs in the third-person plural.

Во́ды_____

Вопросы для обсуждения

1. What is the mood of the poem?

2. How is the arrival of spring represented?

3. How are the spring waters described?

4. Pushkin's favorite season was fall; Tyutchev's was spring. What is your favorite season and why?

5. Tell a little about the arrival of spring in your hometown. Is it similar to the description in the poem or not?

Весéнняя грозá ** (1828)

Люблю́ **грозу́** в нача́ле ма́я,	грозá – thunderstorm
Когда́ весéнний, пéрвый **гром,**	гром – thunder
Как бы резвя́ся и игра́я,	как бы – as if; резвя́ся – frolicking; игра́я – playing
Грохо́чет в нéбе голубо́м.	грохота́ть *(Impf.)* – to rumble; нéбо – sky
Гремя́т раска́ты молоды́е!	греме́ть *(Impf.)* – to thunder; раска́т – peal
Вот **до́ждик бры́знул, пыль** лети́т . . .	до́ждик *(dim.)* – дождь – rain; бры́знуть *(Perf.)* – to drizzle; пыль (f.) – dust
Пови́сли пéрлы дождевы́е,	пови́снуть *(Perf.)* – to hang; пéрл – pearl
И со́лнце **ни́ти золоти́т** . . .	ни́ть – thread; золоти́ть *(Impf.)* – to gild
С **горы́** бежи́т **пото́к прово́рный,**	горá – mountain; пото́к – torrent; прово́рный – fast
В лесу́ не **мо́лкнет** пти́чий **гам,**	мо́лкнуть – to grow silent; пти́чий – bird's; гам – clamor
И гам лесно́й, и **шум наго́рный** –	шум – noise, racket; наго́рный – mountaineous
Всё **вто́рит** вéсело грома́м . . .	вто́рить *(+ D.; Impf.)* – to echo
Ты ска́жешь: **вéтреная Гéба,**	вéтреный – *here:* carefree; Гéба – Hebe

Кормя́ Зеве́сова орла́,

Feeding the eagle of Zeus

Громокипя́щий ку́бок с не́ба,

громокипя́щий – thunder-foaming; ку́бок – chalice

Смея́сь, на зе́млю пролила́!

земля́ – earth; проли́ть *(Perf.)* – to spill

Лексика и грамматика

1. List the nouns from which the following adjectives are formed and give their meaning in

English: весе́нний _____

дождево́й _____

лесно́й _____

наго́рный _____

пти́чий _____

ве́треный _____

2. What is the root in "вто́рить"? What is its meaning in English? _____. Can you

think of any other words with the same root?_____

_____

3. Гром – греме́ть – громокипя́щий have a common root. Find the root and write down its

meaning in English. _____. Make up two sentences with these words.

_____

_____

4. Find the Imperfective gerunds in the poem (3) and list the verbs from which these gerunds are

formed. _____

1. How does the poet describe a spring thunderstorm?

2. What are some color epithets that are used in the poem?

3. Do some research on the Internet and find the mythological story about Hebe and Zeus's eagle.

После́дняя любо́вь ** (1852)

This poem is dedicated to Yelena Denisyeva, whom Tyutchev met when he was forty-seven years old and she was twenty-one. Tyutchev and Yelena fell passionately in love, although Tyutchev remained married to Ernestine. When in 1851 their affair became known, Yelena's father renounced and disinherited his daughter, and her aunt lost her position at the Smolny Institute, the elite boarding school for daughters of noble families where Yelena and Tyutchev's daughters were students. Despite the public ostracism, their turbulent relationship continued for fifteen years until Yelena's death from tuberculosis in 1864. The poems that Tyutchev wrote to Denisyeva—the so –called "Дени́сьевский цикл"—represent a very important part of his poetic legacy. This poem is considered to be emblematic of the whole cycle.

О, как на скло́не на́ших **лет**	на скло́не лет *(idiom.)* – in one's declining years
Нежне́й мы лю́бим и **суеве́рней** . . .	нежне́й *(comp.* of не́жный) – tender; суеве́рный *(comp.)* – superstitious
Сия́й, сия́й, проща́льный свет	сия́ть *(Impf.)* – to shine; проща́льный – departing; свет – light
Любви́ **после́дней, зари́ вече́рней!**	после́дний – last; вече́рняя заря́ – sunset
Полне́ба обхвати́ла тень,	Полне́ба – half a sky; обхвати́ть *(Perf.)* –to enfold; тень *(f.)* – shadow

Лишь там, на **за́паде, бро́дит сия́нье,** – лишь – only; за́пад – west; броди́ть *(Impf.)* – to wander; сия́нье – glow

Поме́дли, поме́дли, вече́рний день, поме́длить *(Perf.)* – to slow down

Продли́сь, продли́сь, **очарова́нье.** продли́ться *(Perf.)* – to last; очарова́нье – enchantment

Пуска́й **скуде́ет** в **жи́лах кровь,** скуде́ть *(Impf.)* – to be depleted; жи́ла – vein; кровь *(f.)* – blood

Но в **се́рдце** не скуде́ет **не́жность** . . . се́рдце – heart; не́жность *(f.)* – tenderness

О ты, после́дняя любо́вь!

Ты и **блаже́нство, и безнаде́жность.** блаже́нство – bliss; безнаде́жность *(f.)* – hopelessness

Ле́ксика и грамматика

1. Find the roots and define their meaning in "полне́ба." _____

Can you think of any other words containing the first root? List them here. _____

_____

2. Сия́ть – сия́нье share a common root. Find the root and write down its meaning in English.

_____. Make up a sentence with any of these words.

_____

3. Find the root and the prefix in "безнаде́жность" and write down their meanings in English.

_____

Do you know any other words with the same root? List them here. _____

_____

4. List all the third-declension nouns (5). _____

91

Make up three sentences with these words. _____

_____

_____

5. Find all the imperatives in the poem (3). _____

Вопросы для обсуждения

1. What is the mood of the poem?

2. How is the comparison between the beauty of an evening sunset and the last love played out in the poem?

3. According to the poet, how does the nature of love change with the years?

4. What are the feelings that the hero is experiencing?

Она сиде́ла на полу́ . . . ** (1858)

This poem was allegedly written for Ernestine von Dornberg, Tyutchev's second wife, to whom he addressed more than five hundred letters over his lifetime.

Она́ сиде́ла на полу́

И **гру́ду пи́сем разбира́ла** –   гру́да – pile; разбира́ть *(Impf.)* – *here:* to sort, go through

И, как **остьı́вшую золу́,**   остьı́вший – cooled; зола́ *(sg.)* – ashes

Брала́ их в ру́ки и **броса́ла** –   броса́ть *(Impf.)* – to throw, toss

Брала́ знако́мые **листьı́**   лист – leaf; *here:* page

И **чу́дно** так на них **гляде́ла** –   чу́дно – strangely, oddly; гляде́ть *(Impf.)* – *here:* to stare

Как ду́ши смо́трят с **высоты́**	душа́ – soul; высота́ – height
На и́ми **бро́шенное те́ло** . . .	бро́шенный – abandoned; те́ло – body

И ско́лько жи́зни бы́ло тут,	
Невозврати́мо пережи́той –	невозврати́мо – irretrievably; пережи́тый – *here:* bygone
И ско́лько **го́рестных** мину́т,	го́рестный – sorrowful
Любви́ и **ра́дости уби́той** . . .	ра́дость (*f.*) – joy; уби́тый – killed

Стоя́л я мо́лча **в стороне́**	мо́лча – silently; в стороне́ – aside
И **пасть** гото́в был на **коле́ни,** –	пасть (*arch., Perf.*) – to fall; коле́ни – knees
И **стра́шно-гру́стно** ста́ло мне,	стра́шно-гру́стно – terribly sad
Как от **прису́щей** ми́лой **те́ни** . . .	прису́щий – *here:* present; те́нь (*f.*) – shadow

Лексика и грамматика

1. Жизнь – пережи́тый share a common root. Find the root and write down its meaning in

English. _____. Make up two sentences with these words.

_____

_____

2. Броса́ть – бро́шенный share a common root. Find the root and write down its meaning in

English. _____. Make up two sentences with these words.

_____

_____

3. Find the root in "го́рестный." Can you think of any other words with the same root?

_____

Make up a sentence with this word. _____

4. Find all the verbs in the Past tense (9) and list them here. _____

_____

What aspect is used for most of them (7)? _____. Why?_____

_____

5. Make up a sentence with "гляде́ть на" + *Acc.* _____

_____

6. Finish the following sentence: И стра́шно-гру́стно ста́ло мне, когда́_____

_____

Вопросы для обсуждения

1. What was the relationship between the lyric hero and the woman?

2. How did it change?

3. What are the feelings of the lyric hero?

4. What are the main themes of the poem?

Умо́м Росси́ю не поня́ть . . .** (1866)

Although Tyutchev spent more than twenty years of his life working as a diplomat in Germany, in 1844 he returned permanently to Russia. While he admired the achievements of Western civilization, this poem reflects his deep belief that Russia had its own path toward development, different from that of Western countries. Tyutchev was a Slavophile and a nationalist, "за́падник по о́бразу жи́зни, славянофи́л по убежде́нию." He authored several articles devoted to the subject of Russia's unique role in history. Ironically, they were all written in French. You can read more online on the topic of the Westerners and the Slavophiles (за́падники и славянофи́лы) or consult A.Walicki's book on the subject, *The Slavophile Controversy*.

Умо́м Росси́ю **не поня́ть,**	ум – mind; не поня́ть (кому чего) – [it] cannot be understood
Арши́ном о́бщим не изме́рить:	арши́н – *here:* yardstick; о́бщий – common; изме́рить *(Perf.)* – to measure
У ней **осо́бенная стать** –	осо́бенный – particular, special; стать *(f.)* – stature
В Росси́ю мо́жно то́лько **ве́рить**.	ве́рить – to believe

Ле́ксика и грамма́тика:

1. Find the root in "изме́рить" and write down its meaning in English. Make up a sentence with this word. _____

2. "Ве́рить" can be used with the Dative (ве́рить кому) or with the Accusative (ве́рить во что) to describe abstract concepts, as in this poem. Make up a sentence with each construction.

_____

_____

3. The construction of the implied subject in the Dative and the infinitive convey modality. An example of such a usage in this poem is "Умо́м Росси́ю не поня́ть" (Russia cannot be understood by the mind). See also the next poem, "Нам не дано́ предугада́ть. . . ." Finish the following sentence: Мне не поня́ть _____

Вопро́сы для обсужде́ния:

1. What does the poem state about the unique nature of Russia?

2. How do you understand these words?

3. Do you agree or disagree?

Нам не дано́ предугада́ть . . .** (1869)

Нам не дано́ предугада́ть,	нам не дано́ – it is not given to us to; предугада́ть *(Perf.)* – to foresee
Как сло́во на́ше **отзовётся,** –	отозваться *(Perf.)* – to answer, echo
И нам **сочу́вствие** даётся,	сочу́вствие – compassion
Как нам даётся **благода́ть** . . .	благода́ть *(f.)* – grace

Лексика и грамматика

1. Find the prefix and the root in "предугада́ть" and write down their meanings in English.

_____ . Can you think of any other verbs

with the same prefix? _____

2. Find the root in "отозва́ться" and write down its meaning in English. _____

Can you think of any other words with the same root? List them here._____

_____

3. Find the prefix and the root in "сочу́вствие" and write down their meanings in

English._____ . Make up a sentence with "сочу́вствие" or

"сочу́вствовать" (+ *D.*). _____

4. The poem says, "И нам сочувствие даётся" (and compassion is given to us).

Be a poet and create an analogous subjectless sentence using this construction. _____

_____

1. How do you understand the meaning of the poem?

2. What does the poem state about the effects of the future on the spoken word? Do you agree or disagree? Explain your point of view.

Чародейкою Зимою . . . *** (1852)

Чародейкою Зимою	чародейка – sorceress
Околдован, лес стоит –	околдован – spellbound
И под **снежной бахромою**,	снежный – snowy; бахрома – fringe
Неподвижною, немою,	неподвижный – still; немой – mute
Чудной жизнью он **блестит**.	чудный – wondrous; блестеть *(Impf.)* – to sparkle
И стоит он, околдован,	
– Не **мертвец** и не живой –	мертвец – corpse
Сном **волшебным очарован**,	волшебный – magical; очарован – enchanted
Весь **опутан**, весь **окован**	опутан – enlaced; окован – enchained
Легкой **цепью пуховой** . . .	цепь *(f.)* – chain; пуховой – downy
Солнце зимнее ли **мещет**	мещет *(arch.)* – метать *(Impf.)* – to cast
На него свой **луч косой** –	луч – ray; косой – *here:* slanting
В нём ничто не **затрепещет**,	затрепетать *(Perf.)* – to stir, quiver

97

Он весь **вспы́хнет** и **забле́щет**   вспы́хнуть *(Perf.)* – to spark; заблесте́ть *(Perf.)* – to sparkle

Ослепи́тельной красо́й.   ослепи́тельный – dazzling; краса́ *(arch.)* – beauty

Лексика и грамматика

1. Find the prefixes and the root in "неподви́жный" and write down their meanings in English.
_____. Make up a sentence with this word.

_____

2. Блеск – блесте́ть – заблесте́ть – блестя́щий share a common root. Find the root and write

down its meaning in English. _____. Make up two sentences with these words.

_____

3. Краса́ – красота́ – краси́вый share a common root. Find the root and write down its meaning

in English. _____. Make up a sentence with any of these words.

_____

4. Снег – сне́жный – снежи́нка share a common root. Find the root and write down its meaning

in English. _____. Make up a sentence with any of these words.

_____

5. Тре́пет – затрепета́ть – тре́петный share a common root. Find the root and write down its

meaning in English. _____. Make up a sentence with any of these words.

_____

6. List all the passive participles (4) and the verbs from which they are formed. Write down the

meanings of the verbs in English. _____

_____

1. What is the poem about?

2. How does the poet describe a winter forest?

3. Compare this poem with Pushkin's "Зимнее утро" above. What are the similarities and differences between the two?

Silentium! *** (1830)

This poem reflects Tyutchev's deep interest in philosophy. During his time in Munich he met the German Romantic poet Heinrich Heine, with whom he became friends, and the philosopher Friedrich von Schelling, who was then teaching at the University of Munich. These meetings inspired Tyutchev's interest in German *Naturphilosophie*, and it found deep echoes in his poetry.

Молчи, **скрывайся** и **тай**	скрываться *(Impf.)* – to hide; таить *(Impf.)* – to conceal
И **чувства** и **мечты** свои –	чувство – feeling; мечта – dream
Пускай в **душевной** глубине	пускай *(colloq.* from пусть) – let; душевный – *cf.* душа – soul; глубина – depth
Встают и **заходят оне**	заходить *(Perf.)* – *here:* to set; оне *(arch.)* – они
Безмолвно, как **звезды** в ночи, –	безмолвно – silently; звезда – star
Любуйся ими – и молчи.	любоваться (+ *Instr., Impf.*) – to admire
Как **сердцу высказать** себя?	сердце – heart; высказать *(Perf.)* – to express
Другому как понять тебя?	
Поймёт ли он, **чем ты живёшь?**	чем ты живёшь *(idiom.)* – What do you live by?
Мысль изречённая есть **ложь.**	мысль *(f.)* – thought; изречённый – spoken; ложь *(f.)* – lie

Взрыва́я, возмути́шь ключи́, –	взрыва́ть *(Impf.)* – *here:* to dig up; возмути́ть – *here:* to cloud; ключ – *here:* spring
Пита́йся и́ми – и молчи́.	пита́ться (+ *Instr., Impf.*) – to nurture
Лишь жить в себе́ само́м **уме́й** –	лишь – only; уме́ть *(Impf.)* – to know how
Есть **це́лый** мир в душе́ твое́й	це́лый – the whole
Тайнственно-волше́бных дум;	тайнственно-волше́бный – mysteriously magical; дума – thought
Их **оглуши́т нару́жный шум,**	оглуши́ть *(Perf.)* – to deafen; нару́жный – exterior; шум – noise
Дневны́е разгоня́т лучи́, –	дневно́й – day; разогна́ть *(Perf.)* – to disperse; луч – ray
Внима́й их **пе́нью** – и молчи́! . . .	внима́ть *(arch., Impf.)* – to listen; пе́нье – singing

Лексика и грамматика

1. Оглуши́ть – глухо́й – глухота́ share a common root. Find the root and write down its meaning in English. _____. Make up a sentence with any of these words. _____

2. List all the third-declension nouns (3). _____
Make up sentences with these words. _____

_____

3. The poem contains some adjectives formed from nouns: душа́ – душе́вный,

день –дневно́й. You have already seen other examples of such word formation in the preceding

poems: ночь – ночно́й, снег – сне́жный, шум –шу́мный. Find the roots and write down their meaning in English. _____.

Make up a sentence with the words from each pair._____

_____

_____

_____

 4. List all the imperatives in the poem (7). _____

_____

Вопросы для обсуждения

1. How do you understand the title of the poem?

2. What does the poet suggest?

3. Why does the poet privilege silence over the spoken word? Find specific examples in the text. Do you agree or disagree?

4. How do you understand the line "Мысль изречённая есть ложь"?

Афанáсий Афанáсьевич Фет (1820–1892)

In many ways the poetry of Afanasy Fet continues the classical tradition of the Golden Age, represented by Batyushkov, Del'vig, and other poets of the Pushkin circle. His main themes are love, nature, and beauty. Some of his contemporaries criticized his poems for their complete lack of political or social content, accusing him of "creating art for art's sake." Fet's personal characteristics—he was a conservative and a demanding landowner—also presented a stark contrast with his lyrical romantic poetry and were a subject of criticism among the liberal literary circles.

The circumstances around Fet's birth are full of drama. Fet was born in Russia in 1820 to Charlotte Elizabeth Becker. She had left her husband, Johann Foeth, and a young daughter in Germany while seven months pregnant to follow a rich Russian landowner, Afanasy Shenshin, to Russia. Shenshin had been taking a mineral water treatment in the resort town of Darmstadt when he met Charlotte and fell in love with her.

Later Charlotte converted to Russian Orthodoxy, and she and Shenshin got married in 1822. Shenshin adopted the child, and for the early years of his life Afanasy Fet was known as a Shenshin. However, when Fet was fourteen years old, it was discovered that he was not a legal son of Shenshin, so he lost his noble title and privileges. This situation left a deep mark on him, and Fet spent most of his adult life trying to regain his noble status and the right to his name through military service. Eventually, at the age of fifty-three he succeeded, and the tsar granted him noble status and the right to be called Shenshin. But he continued to sign his poems as Fet because it was the name under which he first became known as a poet.

Fet is known as the author of profoundly moving love poems. The great love of his life, Maria Lazich, committed suicide by setting herself on fire because Fet was not able to marry her owing to her lack of fortune. He kept writing her his heartrending poems throughout his life.

Чу́дная карти́на . . . * (1842)

Чу́дная карти́на,	чу́дный – marvelous; карти́на – picture
Как ты **мне родна́**:	мне родна́ – so close to me
Бе́лая **равни́на,**	равни́на – plain
По́лная луна́,	по́лный – full; луна́ – moon
Свет небе́с высо́ких,	свет –light; небеса́ *(pl.)* – sky; высо́кий – high
И блестя́щий снег,	блестя́щий – sparkling, glistening; снег – snow

104

И **сане́й далёких**　　　са́ни – sleigh

Одино́кий бег.　　　одино́кий – lonely; бег – run

Лексика и грамматика

1. Родна́ – родно́й – роди́тели – Ро́дина share a common root. Find the root and write down its
meaning in English. _____. Make up two sentences with any of these words.

_____

_____

2. Find the root in "одино́кий" and write down its meaning in English.

_____

3. In the second line of the first stanza to what does the pronoun "ты" refer?_____

4. List all the adjectives in the poem (8) and write down their meanings in English._____

_____

_____

Make up four sentences with any of these adjectives._____

_____

_____

_____

Вопросы для обсуждения

1. What is the mood of the poem?

2. What does the poem evoke for you?

3. Compare Fet's winter landscape with Pushkin's "Зи́мняя доро́га" above.

О́блаком волни́стым . . . * (1843)

О́блаком волни́стым	о́блако – cloud; волни́стый – undulating
Пыль встаёт вдали́;	пыль *(f.)* – dust; вдали́ – in the distance
Ко́нный и́ли пе́ший –	ко́нный – horseman; пе́ший – pedestrian
Не **видать** в пыли́!	видать *(colloq.)* – to see
Ви́жу: кто-то ска́чет	скака́ть *(Impf.)* – to gallop
На лихо́м коне́.	лихо́й – *here:* gallant; конь – horse
Друг мой, друг далёкий,	
Вспо́мни обо мне!	вспо́мнить *(Perf.)* – to remember

Лексика и грамматика

1. Вдали́ – далёкий share a common root. Find the root and write down its meaning in English.

_____. Make up a sentence with any of these words.

_____

2. Пе́ший –пешко́м –пешехо́д share a common root. Find the root and write down its meaning in English. _____. Make up two sentences with these words. _____

_____

3. Find all the verbs in the poem (5) and list them here. What is their tense?_____

_____

Be a poet and finish the following sentence: Вспо́мни о_____

_____!

Вопросы для обсуждения

1. What is the theme of the poem?

2. Can you guess where the event is taking place? Is it in the city or in the country?

3. In your opinion, whom does the poet address in the last lines: "Друг мой, друг далёкий, / Вспомни обо мне!"?

Поделись живы́ми сна́ми . . .* (1847)

Поделись живы́ми сна́ми,	поделиться (+ *Instr.: Perf.*) – to share; живо́й – vivid; с/о́/н – dream
Говори́ **душе́** мое́й;	душа́ – soul
Что не **вы́скажешь** слова́ми –	вы́сказать *(Perf.)* – to express
Зву́ком на́ душу **наве́й**.	звук – sound; наве́ять *(Perf.) – here:* to call up, evoke

Лексика и грамматика

1. Find all the imperatives in the poem (3) and list them here. Indicate what aspect is used in each instance._____

Make up two imperative phrases using any verbs from the poem._____

_____

2. Вы́сказать – расска́зывать – сказа́ть share a common root. Find the root and write down its meaning in English. _____. Make up two sentences with these words.

Remember that all the verbs with the root "–каз–" will take the Dative. _____

_____

_____

Вопросы для обсуждения

1. What is the theme of the poem?

2. According to the poet, how does music compare to the spoken word?

3. Compare this poem to Tyutchev's *"Silentium!"* Do you find any similarities between the two?

Шёпот, робкое дыханье . . . * (1850)

Шёпот, робкое дыханье,	шёпот – whisper; робкий – timid; дыханье – breath
Трели соловья,	трель *(f.)* – warble; солов/е́/й – nightingale
Серебро и колыханье	серебро – silver; колыханье – swaying
Сонного ручья,	сонный – sleepy; руч/е́/й – brook
Свет ночной, ночны́е **тени,**	свет – light; тень *(f.)* – shadow
Тени без конца,	
Ряд волшебных изменений	ряд – raw; волшебный – magical; изменение – change
Милого лица,	
В **ды́мных ту́чках пу́рпур ро́зы,**	дымный – smoky; тучка – cloud; пурпур – purple
О́тблеск янтаря́,	отблеск – reflection; янтарь – amber

| И **лобза́ния**, и **слёзы**, | лобза́ние *(arch.)* – kiss; слеза́ – tear |
| И **заря́**, заря́! . . . | заря́ – down |

Лексика и грамматика

1. Find all the nouns in the plural appearing in the poem (6)._____

_____

2. Write down all the singular nouns with their corresponding adjectives and indicate the gender of the nouns._____

_____

3. The poet uses the phrase "Ряд волше́бных измене́ний / ми́лого лица́" to describe the changes on the face of his beloved. What else can be described as "волше́бный"? Give two examples._____

4. Find all the uses of the Genitive case (6). _____

_____

Вопросы для обсуждения

1. What is the mood of the poem? Is it happy or sad?

2. What is happening in the poem?

3. How is the poetry of the night described? Find specific examples in the text.

Це́лый мир от красоты́ . . . * (1874)

| **Це́лый мир от красоты́**, | це́лый – the whole; мир – world; красота́ – beauty |
| **От вели́ка и до ма́ла**, | от вели́ка и до ма́ла *(idiom.)* – *here:* both great and small |

| И **напра́сно и́щешь** ты | напра́сно – in vain; иска́ть *(Impf.)* – to look for |
| **Отыска́ть** её **нача́ло**. | отыска́ть *(Perf.)* – to find; нача́ло – beginning |

Что тако́е день **иль век**	что тако́е – what is; иль – или – or; век – century
Перед тем, что **бесконе́чно**?	пе́ред (+ *Instr.*) – before, in front of; бесконе́чно – infinite
Хоть не **ве́чен** челове́к,	хоть – хотя́ – although; ве́чен – eternal; челове́к – human being
То, что ве́чно, – **челове́чно**.	челове́чно – human

Лексика и грамматика

1. Find the root in ве́чен – ве́чно and indicate its meaning in English. _____. Make up a sentence with any of these words_____

_____

2. Челове́к – челове́чно share a common root. Find the root and write down its meaning in English. _____. Make up two sentences with these words._____

_____

3. Иска́ть – и́щешь – отыска́ть share a common root. Find the root and write down its meaning in English. _____. Make up a sentence with one of these words.

_____

4. Пе́ред + *Instr.* means "before, in front of." Make up a sentence with this preposition._____

_____

Вопросы для обсуждения

1. What does the poem assert? Do you agree or disagree?

2. How do you understand the last lines: "Хоть не вечен человек, / Всё, что вечно, человечно"?

Я пришёл к тебе с приветом . . . ** (1843)

Я пришёл к тебе с **приветом**,	привет – greeting
Рассказать, что **солнце встало**,	солнце – sun; встать *(Perf.)* – to rise
Что оно **горячим светом**	горячий – hot; свет – light
По **листам затрепетало**;	лист – leaf; затрепетать *(Perf.)* – *here:* to quiver
Рассказать, что **лес проснулся**,	лес – forest; проснуться *(Perf.)* – to wake up
Весь проснулся, **веткой** каждой,	весь – the whole; ветка – twig
Каждой **птицей встрепенулся**	птица – bird; встрепенуться *(Perf.)* – to shudder
И весенней **полон жаждой**;	полон *(+ Instr.)* – full; жажда – thirst
Рассказать, что с той же **страстью**,	страсть *(f.)* – passion
Как вчера, пришёл я **снова**,	снова – again
Что душа всё так же счастью	
И тебе **служить** готова;	служить *(+ D.; Impf.)* – to serve
Рассказать, что **отовсюду**	отовсюду – from everywhere
На меня **весельем веет**,	веселье – gaiety, cheer; веять *(poet., Impf.)* – to waft

111

Что не зна́ю сам, что́ бу́ду

Петь – но то́лько **пе́сня зре́ет.** петь *(Impf.)* – to sing; пе́сня – song; зре́ть *(Impf.)* – to ripen

Лексика и грамматика

1. Find the root in "сно́ва" and write down its meaning in English. _____. Can

you think of any other words with the same root? List them here._____

_____ . Make up a sentence with "сно́ва."

_____

2. Петь –пе́сня share a common root. Find the root and write down its meaning in English.

_____. Make up two sentences with these words.

_____

_____

3. Find all the examples of the Dative case (4). _____

_____

4. Look at the third stanza of the poem. "Служи́ть + *D*." means " to serve," and the soul of the

poet is ready to serve happiness and his love. Make up a sentence using "служи́ть."_____

_____

5. Finish the following sentence: Я пришёл/пришла́ рассказа́ть тебе́, что_____

_____

Вопросы для обсуждения

1. What is the tone of the poem?

2. What does the lyric hero want to say to his beloved?

3. What is the connection between the spring awakening of the forest and the soul in love?

Офе́лия ги́бла и пе́ла . . . ** (1846)

Офе́лия ги́бла и пе́ла,

Офе́лия – Ophelia; ги́бнуть *(Impf.)* – to perish

И пе́ла, сплета́я венки́;

сплета́ть *(Impf.)* – to weave; вен/о́/к – wreath

С цвета́ми, венка́ми и пе́снью

пе́снью *(Instr. of arch.* песнь) *(f.)* – song

На дно опусти́лась реки́.

дно – bottom; опусти́ться – to go down

И мно́гое с пе́снями ка́нет

ка́нуть *(Perf.)* – to fall, sink

Мне в ду́шу на тёмное дно,

тёмный – dark

И мно́го мне чу́вства, и пе́сен,

чу́вство – feeling

И слёз, и мечта́ний дано́.

слёзы – tears; мечта́ние *(arch.)* – dream

Ле́ксика и грамма́тика:

1. Look at the verbs in the first stanza. List them here and indicate their tense and aspect. Explain the aspectual choice.

_____

_____

2. Find all the uses of the Genitive case (5) and write them down. _____

_____. Make up a sentence using "мно́го."

_____

3. Find all the uses of the Instrumental case (4) and write them down. _____

Make up a sentence with "с цвета́ми." _____

4. Find the subject in the second stanza, "И мно́гое с пе́снями ка́нет / Мне в ду́шу на тёмное

дно." _____

5. What is the subject in the last sentence, "И мно́го мне чу́вства, и пе́сен, / И слёз, и

мечта́ний дано́"? _____

Вопросы для обсуждения

1. What do you think the poem is about?

2. How is the metaphor of the bottom of the river and the depths of the soul presented in the
poem?

3. How do you understand the last lines, "И мно́гое с пе́снями ка́нет / Мне в ду́шу на тёмное
дно, / И мно́го мне чу́вства, и пе́сен, / И слёз, и мечта́ний дано́"?

Я тебе́ ничего́ не скажу́ . . . ** (1885)

Я тебе́ ничего́ не скажу́,

И тебя́ не **встрево́жу ничу́ть,** встрево́жить *(Perf.)* – to alarm; ничу́ть – not at all

И о том, что́ я мо́лча твержу́, мо́лча – silently; тверди́ть *(Impf.)* – to repeat

Не **решу́сь ни за что́ намекну́ть.** реши́ться *(Perf.)* – to dare; ни за что – not for anything; намекну́ть

(Perf.) – to hint

Це́лый день спят ночны́е цветы́,

114

Но **лишь** со́лнце за **ро́щу зайдёт,** лишь – *here:* as soon as; ро́ща – grove; зайти́ – *here:* to go down

Раскрыва́ются ти́хо **листы́** раскрыва́ться *(Impf.)* – to open; листы́ – leaves

И я слы́шу, как **се́рдце цветёт.** се́рдце – heart; цвести́ *(Impf.)* – to blossom

И в больну́ю, уста́лую **грудь** грудь *(f.)* – chest

Ве́ет вла́гой ночно́й . . . я **дрожу́,** ве́ять *(Impf.)* – to whiff; вла́га – moisture; дрожа́ть – to tremble

Я тебя́ не встрево́жу ничу́ть,

Я тебе́ ничего́ не скажу́.

Лексика и грамматика

1. Мо́лча – молча́ние – молча́ть share a common root. Find the root and write down its

meaning in English. _____. Make up a sentence with any

of these words._____

2. In the first stanza the poet uses the idiomatic expression "ни за что́" (not for anything).

Be a poet and finish the following sentence (remember that the verb must be negated in Russian):

Я ни за что́_____

Вопросы для обсуждения

1. What is the poem about?

2. What does the lyric hero not want to say? Why do you think he says "Я тебе́ ничего́ не
   скажу́"?

3. How do his feelings change at nightfall? Why?

4. Is it a happy poem or a sad poem? Explain your point of view.

Учи́сь у них, у ду́ба, у берёзы . . . ** (1883)

Учи́сь у них – у ду́ба, у берёзы.	ду́б – oak; берёза – birch
Круго́м зима́. Жесто́кая пора́!	круго́м – around; жесто́кий – cruel; пора́ – time
Напра́сные на них засты́ли слёзы,	напра́сный – in vain; засты́ть (Perf.) – to freeze; слёзы – tears
И тре́снула, сжима́яся, кора́.	тре́снуть (Perf.) – to crack; сжима́яся – shrinking; кора́ – bark
Всё злей мете́ль и с ка́ждою мину́той	всё злей – getting more and more angry; мете́ль (f.) – blizzard
Серди́то рвёт после́дние листы́,	серди́то – angrily; рвать (Impf.) – here: to break off; после́дний – last; листы́ – leaves
И за́ сердце хвата́ет хо́лод лю́тый;	се́рдце – heart; хвата́ть (Impf.) – to seize; хо́лод – cold; лю́тый – fierce
Они́ стоя́т, молча́т; молчи́ и ты!	молча́ть (Impf.) – to be silent
Но верь весне́. Её промчи́тся ге́ний,	промча́ться (Perf.) – to rush by; ге́ний – genius
Опя́ть тепло́м и жи́знию дыша́.	тепло́ – warmth; жи́знию (arch.) – жизнью; дыша́ – breathing
Для я́сных дней, для но́вых открове́ний	я́сный – clear; открове́ние – revelation
Переболи́т скорбя́щая душа́.	переболе́ть (Perf.) – to suffer through; скорбя́щий – grieving

Лексика и грамматика

1. Find the root in "откровéние" and write down its meaning in English. _____. Can you think of any other words with the same root?_____

2. Find the root and the prefix in "переболéть" and write down their meanings in English._____

_____ . What does "переболéть + *Instr.*" literally mean? What other words with the same root do you know? _____

Make up a sentence with any of the words with the same root._____

_____

3. Find all the imperatives in the poem (3)._____

_____ . Make up two sentences with these

verbs._____

_____

Вопросы для обсуждения

1. In your opinion, what is the poem about?

2. How is the metaphor of winter and spring played out in the poem?

3. How does the mood of the poem change between the first and the last stanza? Does the poem end on a happy or sad note?

Какие-то нóсятся звýки . . . *** (1853)

Какие-то **нóсятся звýки**	носúться *(Impf.)* – *here:* to float; звýк – sound
И **льнут** к моемý **изголóвью.**	льнуть *(Impf.)* – to cling; изголóвье – headboard

Полны́ они **то́мной разлу́ки,**	полны́ – full of; то́мный – languorous; разлу́ка – parting
Дрожа́т небыва́лой любо́вью.	дрожа́ть *(Impf.)* – to tremble; небыва́лый – unheard of
Каза́лось бы, что ж? **Отзвуча́ла**	каза́лось бы – it would seem to be; отзвуча́ть *(Perf.)* – to stop resounding
После́дняя не́жная ла́ска,	после́дний – last; не́жный – tender; ла́ска – caress
По у́лице **пыль** пробежа́ла,	пыль *(f.)* – dust; пробежа́ть *(Perf.) – here:* to pass through
Почто́вая скры́лась коля́ска . . .	почто́вая коля́ска – postal carriage; скры́ться *(Perf.)* – to disappear
И то́лько . . . Но пе́сня разлу́ки	И то́лько – *here:* and that's it
Несбы́точной **дра́знит** любо́вью,	несбы́точный – impossible, unreal; дразни́ть *(Impf.)* – to tease
И но́сятся **све́тлые** зву́ки	све́тлый – light
И льнут к моему́ изголо́вью.	

Лексика и грамматика

1. Find the root and the prefix in "небыва́лый" and "несбы́точный" and write down their meanings in English. _____. Can you think of any other words with the same root?_____

Make up a sentence with any of these words._____

_____

2. Изголо́вье – голова́ – глава́ – загла́вный share a common root. Find the root and write down its meaning in English. _____

Make up two sentences with any of these words. _____

_____

_____

3. Find the root and the prefix in "отзвучáть" and write down their meanings in English.

_____. Can you think of any other words with the same

root? _____. Make up a sentence with one of these words.

_____

4. Be a poet and finish the following sentence: Казáлось бы, _____

_____

Вопросы для обсуждения

1. What is the poem about?

2. What is the mood of the poem?

3. What can be inferred about the power of music and its effect on human emotions? Do you
agree or disagree with the poet?

Что за ночь! Прозрáчный вóздух скóван . . . *** (1854)

Что за ночь! **Прозрáчный вóздух скóван**; прозрáчный – transparent; вóздух – air, скóван – *here:*

motionless, still

Над землёй **клубúтся аромáт**.   клубúться *(Impf.)* – to swirl; аромáт – aroma

О, тепéрь я счáстлив, я **взволнóван,**   взволнóван – excited

О, тепéрь я **вы́сказаться** рад!   вы́сказаться *(Perf.)* – to declare/express oneself

119

Пóмнишь час послéднего **свидáнья**!   свидáнье – date, rendezvous

Безотрáден сýмрак нóчи был;   безотрáден – dreary, desolate; сýмрак – twilight

Ты ждалá, ты **жáждала признáнья** –   жáждать *(Impf.)* – to thirst; признáнье – *here:* declaration

Я молчáл: тебя я не любил.

Холодéла кровь, и сéрдце **ныло:**   холодéть *(Impf.)* – to grow cold; кровь *(f.)* – blood; ныть

    (Impf.) – to ache

Так **тяжкá** былá твоя **печáль**;   тяжкá – heavy; печáль *(f.)* – sadness

Гóрько мне за нас обóих было,   гóрько – bitter

И сказáть мне прáвду было жаль.

Но тепéрь, когда **дрожý** и **млéю**   дрожáть *(Impf.)* – to tremble; млéть *(Impf.)* – to be overcome

И, как **раб**, твой кáждый **взор ловлю́,**   раб – slave; взор – glance; ловить *(Impf.)* – to catch

Я не лгу, **назвáв тебя своéю**   лгать *(+ D.; Impf.)* – to lie; назвáв тебя своéю – having

    called you mine

И **кляня́сь**, что я тебя люблю́!   кляня́сь – vowing

Лéксика и граммáтика:

1. Find the root and the prefix in "вы́сказаться" and write down their meanings in English.

_____. Can you think of any other words with the same

root?_____

Make up a sentence with this verb. _____

2. Безотра́ден – рад – ра́дость – ра́доваться (+ *D.*) share a common root. Find the root and

indicate its meaning in English. _____

Make up two sentences with any of these words. _____

_____

3. Reread the second and third stanzas and list all the verbs pertaining to the feelings of the poet

in the past: я _____, and the woman to

whom he is writing: ты _____

Find all the verbs describing the poet's emotions at present: но тепе́рь я _____

_____

Вопросы для обсуждения:

1. How does the mood of the poem change over the course of the story?

2. Whom does the lyric hero address?

3. How does he compare the two dates?

4. How have his feelings changed?

Ещё ма́йская ночь *** (1857)

Кака́я ночь! На всём кака́я **не́га**!　　　　не́га – bliss

Благодарю́, родно́й полно́чный край!　　благодари́ть *(Impf.)* – to thank; родно́й – native;

полно́чный – midnight; край – *here:* land

121

Из **ца́рства** льдов, из ца́рства **вьюг** и сне́га	ца́рство – kingdom; льдов – л/ё/д – ice; вьюга – snowstorm, blizzard
Как **свеж** и **чист** твой **вылета́ет** май!	свеж – све́жий – fresh; чист – чи́стый – pure; вылета́ть *(Impf.)* – to fly out
Кака́я ночь! **Все звёзды до еди́ной**	все до еди́ной *(idiom.)* – down to the last one
Тепло́ и кро́тко в ду́шу смо́трят вновь,	тепло́ – warmly; кро́тко – gently
И в **во́здухе** за пе́снью **соловьи́ной**	во́здух – air; соловьи́ный – of nightingale
Разно́сится тревога и любо́вь.	разноси́ться *(Impf.)* – to spread; тревога – *here:* agitation
Берёзы ждут. Их **лист полупрозра́чный**	берёза – birch; лист – leaf; полупрозра́чный – semitransparent
Засте́нчиво мани́т и **те́шит взор.**	засте́нчиво – shyly; мани́ть *(Impf.)* – to lure, те́шить *(Impf.)* – to please, gratify; взор *(poet.)* – eyes
Они́ **дрожа́т.** Так де́ве **новобра́чной**	дрожа́ть *(Impf.)* – to tremble; новобра́чная де́ва *(poet.)* – bride
И **ра́достен** и чужд её **убо́р.**	ра́достен – joyful; чужд – strange; убо́р *(arch.)* – dress
Нет, никогда́ **нежне́й** и **бестеле́сней**	нежне́й – more tenderly; бестеле́сней – more incorporeally

Твой **лик,** о ночь, не мог меня́ **томи́ть!**   лик *(arch.)* – face; томи́ть *(Impf.)* – to torment

Опя́ть к тебе́ иду́ с **нево́льной** пе́сней,   нево́льный – involuntary

Нево́льной – и **после́дней,** может быть.   после́дний – last

Лексика и грамматика

1. Find the root in "родно́й" and write down its meaning in English._____

What other words with the same root do you know?_____

_____

 Make up a sentence with родно́й."_____

_____

2. Find the root and the prefix in "вылета́ть" and write down their meanings in English._____

_____. Make up a sentence with this word.

_____

3. Find the root and the prefix in "нево́льный" and write down their meanings in English._____

_____. Make up a sentence with this word.

_____

4. List all the short-form adjectives(4)._____

_____. Make up two sentences with any of these

adjectives._____

_____

Вопросы для обсуждения

1. What is the mood of the poem?

2. How does the poet describe the May night? Find specific examples in the text.

3. Why is May described as "вылетáет"? What imagery does the verb evoke?

4. How do you understand the line "Опя́ть к тебé иду́ с невóльной пéсней"? Why "невóльной"?

Сия́ла ночь. Луно́й был пóлон сад . . . *** (1877)

According to the recollections of Tatyana Andreevna Kuz'minskaya, Lev Tolstoy's sister-in-law, this poem was inspired by an occasion when Fet and his wife were guests at Tolstoy's estate and were listening to young Tatyana's singing. Ten years later Fet heard her singing again, remembered his earlier impression, and wrote the poem.

Сия́ла ночь. **Луно́й** был **пóлон** сад. Лежáли	сия́ть – to shine; луна́ – moon; пóлон – full
Лучи́ у нáших **ног** в **гости́ной** без **огнéй.**	луч – ray; нога́ – foot; гости́ная – sitting room; огóнь – fire
Роя́ль был весь **раскры́т**, и **стру́ны** в нём **дрожáли,**	роя́ль – grand piano; раскры́т – open; струна́ – string; дрожáть *(Impf.)* – to tremble
Как и **сердца́** у нас за **пéснию** твоéй.	сéрдце – heart; пéсня – song
Ты пéла до **зари́**, в **слезáх изнемогáя,**	заря́ – down; слеза́ – tear; изнемогáть *(Impf.)* – to languish
Что ты одна́ – любóвь, что нет любви́ **инóй,**	инóй – other
И так хотéлось жить, чтоб, **зву́ка** не **роня́я,**	звук – sound; роня́ть (Impf.) – to drop
Тебя люби́ть, **обня́ть** и **плáкать** над тобóй.	обня́ть *(Impf.)* – to embrace; плáкать *(Impf.)* – to cry
И мнóго лет прошлó, **томи́тельных** и ску́чных,	томи́тельный – wearying
И вот в **тиши́** ночнóй твой гóлос слы́шу вновь,	тишь *(f.)* – тишина́ – silence

124

И **ве́ет**, как тогда́, во **вздо́хах** э́тих **зву́чных**, ве́ять *(poet.)* – to waft; вздох – sigh; зву́чный –

audible

Что ты одна́ – вся жизнь, что ты одна́ – любо́вь.

Что нет **обид судьбы́** и се́рдца **жгу́чей му́ки**, оби́да – offense; судьба́ – fate; жгу́чий – burning,

му́ка – torment

А жи́зни нет конца́, и **це́ли** нет ино́й, цель *(f.)* – goal

Как то́лько **ве́ровать** в **рыда́ющие** зву́ки, ве́ровать *(eccl.)* – to believe; рыда́ющий – sobbing

Тебя́ люби́ть, обня́ть и пла́кать над тобо́й!

Лексика и грамматика

1. List all the third-declension nouns (5). _____

_____

Make up three sentences with thesewords. _____

_____

_____

2. List all the infinitives in the poem (4) and write down their aspect. _____

_____

Make up two sentences with these verbs. _____

_____

_____

3. Find the passive participles (2) and gerunds (2) in the poem and write down the verbs from which they are formed._____

_____

4. In the last stanza the poet says, "А жи́зни [Д] нет конца́" (And there is no end to life). Make up a sentence using the expression "нет конца́." Remember to put the subject in the Dative.

_____

Вопросы для обсуждения

1. What two events does the poem mention?

2. How does the poet describe the power of music? What is the connection between music and love?

3. Does time affect the feelings of a lyric hero? Cite an example from the poem.

4. Compare this poem with Pushkin's "Я по́мню чу́дное мгнове́нье" above. What do they have in common, and how are they different?

Инноке́нтий Фёдорович А́нненский (1856–1909)

Innokenty Annensky is known as a poet, literary critic, playwright, translator, philologist, and scholar of antiquity. Like Tyutchev, who had a long and prominent career as a statesman and considered his poetry secondary to his main occupation, during his lifetime Annensky was indifferent to the success of his poems and only published one book, *Ти́хие пе́сни* (Quiet Songs), in 1904, signed with the pen name of Nik. T-o. Significantly, he chose this pen name because it contains a play on words meaning "nobody" in Russian.

After his graduation from the Department of History and Philology at St. Petersburg University, Annensky worked for several years as an instructor of Ancient Greek and Latin and Russian literature at the Gurevich Lycée in St. Petersburg. He then served as a director of several high schools.

It is significant that Annensky was the director of the Tsarkoselsky Gymnasium in 1896–1906 when another poet, Nikolai Gumilev, was a pupil there, and it was to Annensky that Gumilev showed his first poems.

Annensky's poetry continues the great tradition of Baratynsky, Tyutchev, and Fet. One literary critic, A. Gisetti, called Annesky a "поэт мировóй дисгармóнии" (a poet of world disharmony) because at the center of his poetry lay the unresolved conflict between dream and reality and between day and night, and even the human soul itself is torn by conflicting impulses. There is an ongoing motive of the tragic solitude of a lyric hero and a dream of unattainable harmony that leads to tension and dissonance in his poetric world. Annensky is considered a pre-Symbolist and a predecessor of Blok, Akhmatova, Pasternak, Gumilev, and several other major Symbolist poets. Anna Akhmatova was a great admirer of Annensky's poems.

Another of Annensky's literary contributions was his extensively annotated translation of the complete works of Euripides, to which he devoted more than fifteen years of his life. He also wrote four plays set in antiquity in the style of Euripides. In addition to his numerous translations of classical Greek and Roman authors, Annensky translated into Russian the French Symbolist poets Baudlaire, Verlaine, Rimbaud, and Mallarmé. In 1909 Annensky's life was tragically cut short by a heart attack at the age of fifty-four. The poems included below are from a book published posthumously under the title of *Кипарúсовый Ларéц* (Cypress chest). The title refers to a cypress chest in which Annensky kept his manuscripts.

Среди миров ** (1901)

Среди миров, в мерцании светил   среди (+ *G.*) – among; миры – *here:* galaxies; мерцание –

scintillation; светило – planet

Одной Звезды я **повторяю** имя . . .   повторять *(Impf.)* – to repeat

Не потому, чтоб я Её любил,   не потому, чтоб – not because . . .

А потому, что я **томлюсь** с другими.   томиться *(Impf.)* – to languish

И если мне **сомненье тяжело**,   сомненье – doubt; тяжело – heavy

Я у Неё одной **ищу** ответа,   искать *(Impf.)* – to look for

Не потому, что от Неё **светло**,   светло – light

А потому, что **с Ней не надо света**.   с Ней не надо света – with Her there is no need for light

Лексика и грамматика

1. Find the root in "повторять" and write down its meaning in English. Can you think of any

other words with the same root?_____

Make up a sentence with this word._____

2. Светло – свет – светлый – светило share a common root. Find the root and write down its

meaning in English. _____. Make up two sentences with these

words._____

_____

3. List all the verbs in the present tense (3)._____

4. "Искать" can be used with the Accusative for specific things (e.g., я ищу́ уче́бник по ру́сскому) or with the Genitive for abstract concepts, as in this poem, and as in Lermontov's "Выхожу́ оди́н я на доро́гу . . ." above: "Я ищу́ свобо́ды и поко́я. . . ." Make up a sentence with each usage. _____

_____

_____

Вопросы для обсуждения:

1. What do you think the poem is about?

2. What is the mood of the poem?

3. How do you understand the last lines of the poem, "Не потому́, что от Неё светло́ / а потому́, что с Ней не на́до све́та"?

Я ду́мал, что се́рдце из ка́мня . . . ** (1910)

Я ду́мал, что **се́рдце** из **ка́мня**,	се́рдце – heart; ка́м/е/нь – stone
Что **пу́сто** оно и **мертво́**:	пу́сто – empty; мертво́ – dead
Пусть в **се́рдце** ого́нь языка́ми	ого́нь – fire; язы́к – tongue
Похо́дит – ему́ ничего́.	похо́дить *(Perf.)* – to go for a while; ему́ ничего́ *(idiom.)* – nothing [will happen] to it
И **то́чно: мне бы́ло не бо́льно,**	то́чно – *here:* indeed; мне бы́ло не бо́льно – it did not hurt
А бо́льно, так **ра́зве чуть-чуть.**	ра́зве чуть-чуть – only a little bit
И всё-таки лу́чше **дово́льно,**	всё-таки – still; дово́льно – enough

Заду́й, пока́ мо́жно **заду́ть** . . .   заду́й – *(Impf.* of заду́ть *[Perf.])* – to blow out; пока́ – while

На се́рдце темно́, как в моги́ле,   темно́ – dark; моги́ла – grave

Я знал, что **пожа́р я уйму́** . . .   пожа́р – fire; уня́ть *(Perf.)* – *here:* to stop

Ну вот . . . и ого́нь **потуши́ли,**   ну вот – and here we are; потуши́ть *(Perf.)* – to extinguish

А я умира́ю в **дыму́.**   дым – smoke

Лексика и грамматика

1. Find the prefix and the root in "походи́ть" and write down their meanings in English.

_____

In this instance the prefix "по–" limits activity in time. Can you come up with other verbs where that prefix has the same function? (Hint: the starting non-prefixed forms have to be Imperfective, and they have to describe activities.) _____

_____

Make up two sentences with these verbs._____

_____

2. "Се́рдце из ка́мня" is a poetic metaphor stating that the heart is made of stone. The same construction is used literally to describe what things are made of—for example, стул из де́рева, кольцо́ из зо́лота, нож из серебра́. Make up a sentence with this construction._____

_____

3. In the second stanza we read "Мне бы́ло не бо́льно." Remember that in Russian a Dative subject + adverb is used to express a physical or emotional state—for example, мне гру́стно, мне хо́лодно, нам бы́ло ве́село. Make up two sentences with this construction._____

_____

_____

Вопросы для обсуждения

1. What is the poem about?

2. How does the poet describe what was happening to the heart?

3. How do you understand the lines "Пусть в се́рдце ого́нь языка́ми / Похо́дит – ему́ ничего́"?

4. How do you understand the ending: "Ну вот . . . и ого́нь потуши́ли, / А я умира́ю в дыму́"?

5. In your own words write down the main theme of the poem._____

Он и я *** (1910)

Давно́ **меж ли́стьев налили́сь**	меж *(poet.)* – among; ли́стья – leaves; нали́ться *(Perf.)* – *here:* to be filled
Исто́мой ро́зовой **тюльпа́ны**,	исто́ма – languor; тюльпа́н – tulip
Но **стра́стно в су́мрачную высь**	стра́стно – passionately; су́мрачный – twilight; высь *(f.)* – height
Ухо́дит **ро́кот** фортепья́нный.	ро́кот – roar
И **му́ка** там **иль торжество́**,	му́ка – torment; иль *(poet.)* – или – or; торжество́ – triumph
Разоблаче́нье иль **зага́дка**,	разоблаче́нье – revelation; зага́дка – enigma

Но Он – ничей, а вы – его,

И вам **сознанье** это **сладко**. сознанье – *here:* feeling; сладко – sweet

А я **лучей иной звезды** луч – ray; иной *(poet.)* – different; звезда – star

Ищу в **сомненьи** и **тревожно**, сомненье – doubt; тревожно – anxiously

Я, как **настройщик**, все **лады** настройщик – tuner; лады – keys

Перебираю осторожно. перебирать *(Impf.)* – to go through; осторожно – carefully

Темнеет . . . Комната **пуста** темнеть *(Impf.)* – to grow dark; пуст – empty

С трудом я вспоминаю что-то, с трудом *(idiom.)* – with difficulty

И **безответна, хоть чиста**, безответ/е/н – non-responsive; хоть – хотя – although; чиста – pure

За нотой умирает **нота**. За нотой . . . нота – note after note

Лексика и грамматика

1. Высь – невысокий – высота share a common root. Find the root and write down its meaning

in English. _____. Make up a sentence with any of these words.

_____

2. Find the prefix and the root in "безответный" and write down their meanings in English.

_____. Can you think of any other words with the same root?

Make up a sentence with "безответный."_____

_____

3. In the last stanza we read, "за но́той умира́ет но́та." This is an idiomatic construction that is frequently used in time expressions—for example, день за днём, час за ча́сом, год за го́дом. Make up a sentence with any of these expressions. _____

_____

It is also used in the idiomatic expression "друг за дру́гом" (one after another). Make up a sentence with "друг за ру́гом." _____

Вопросы для обсуждения

1. What is the poem about?

2. In the second line, "Но Он – ниче́й, а вы – его́," to what does "Он" refer?

3. In your opinion, why is the poem called "Он и я"?

Алекса́ндр Алекса́ндрович Блок (1880–1921)

Alexander Blok is closely associated with the Symbolist movement. He is often compared to

Pushkin because of his leading role among the poets of the Silver Age and his enormous

influence on subsequent poets. Many leading poets of the Silver Age, such as Marina Tsvetaeva,

Anna Akhmatova, Boris Pasternak, and Vladimir Nabokov, wrote poetic tributes to Blok.

Blok was born into a prominent intellectual family in St. Petersburg and wrote his first poem at

the age of five. He graduated from St. Petersburg University's Department of History and

Philology. His first collection of poems, titled *Poems about a Beautiful Lady (Стихи́ о

Прекра́сной Да́ме),* was dedicated to his future wife, Lyubov Mendeleeva, the daughter of a

famous chemist, Dmitry Mendeleev, whose name is associated with the creation of the Table of

Elements. This collection was published in 1904 to great acclaim.

Blok's poetic reputation only grew with the publication of two subsequent collections of poems, *Inadvertent Joy (Нечáянная рáдость)* and *Mask of Snow (Снéжная Мáска)* in 1907.

From his early years Blok was deeply interested in the theater. He played in amateur shows at Shakhmatovo, Blok's family estate, where he used to spend the summers, and even wanted to become professional actor when he was young. His lifelong passion for the theater was reflected in his works and his life (see his poetic cycles *Faina* and *Mask of Snow*, dedicated to a talented and beautiful actress of the Komissarzhevsky Theater, Natalya Volokhova, and *Carmen,* dedicated to an opera singer, Lyubov Del'mas). He wrote several plays and participated in the staging of several of his dramas— among them *The Puppet Show (Балагáнчик)* directed by Vsevolod Meyerhold at Komissarzhevsky Theater and *The Unknown Woman (Незнакóмка).* Blok's later play *The Rose and the Cross (Рóза и Крест)* was favorably received by Stanislavsky and the play was in rehearsals at Stanislavsky's Moscow Art Theater when the February revolution of 1917 interrupted this work. Blok's wife Lyubov Mendeleeva also became an actress and performed at Vsevolod Meyerhold theater and other professional companies.

Like many other poets of his time, Blok enthusiastically supported the October Revolution of 1917 and decided to remain in Russia and work for the new government. He saw the revolution as the symbolic collapse of the bourgois world, with its corrupt values, and an exciting opportunity for new beginings. His symbolic poem "The Twelve" («Двенáдцать») was written in 1918 as a response to the revolution and reflected his beliefs at that time. However, by 1921

Blok was disillusioned with the new system. His health deteriorated and he died in Petrograd on August 7, 1921.

One of Blok's last public appearances was a speech that he delivered at the House of Writers on the eighty-fourth anniversary of Pushkin's death, "О назначе́нии поэ́та" (On the Poet's Calling); it was triumphantly received and is viewed as his poetic testament. In his speech Blok tries to answer the question "What is a poet?" and he says, "поэт – сын гармо́нии; ему́ дана́ кака́я-то роль в мирово́й культу́ре. Три де́ла возло́жены на него́: во-пе́рвых, освободи́ть зву́ки из родно́й, безнача́льной стихи́и, в кото́рой они́ пребыва́ют; во-вторы́х, – привести́ эти зву́ки в гармо́нию, дать им фо́рму, в-тре́тьих, – внести́ эту гармо́нию во вне́шний мир. (A poet is the son of harmony; such a role is given to him in world culture. Three tasks are entrusted to him: first, to liberate sounds from the native eternal element in which they dwell; second, to bring these sounds into harmony, to give them form; third, to bring this harmony into the external world (cited in К. Мочу́льский, "Алекса́ндр Блок. Андре́й Бе́лый. Вале́рий Брю́сов"; Moscow, Респу́блика, 1997, p. 250) Although Blok was speaking on Pushkin and his poetry, these words are equally applicable to his own poetic worldview, and one can say that the three lofty tasks of a poet have been splendidly fulfilled in Blok's poetic legacy.

Ночь, у́лица, фона́рь, апте́ка . . . * (1912)

Ночь, у́лица, **фона́рь, апте́ка,**	фона́рь – street lamp; апте́ка – drugstore
Бессмы́сленный и **ту́склый свет.**	бессмы́сленный – senseless; ту́склый – dim; свет – light

139

Живи́ ещё хоть че́тверть ве́ка –

ещё – still; хоть – even; че́тверть – quarter; ве́к – century

Всё бу́дет так. Исхо́да нет.

исхо́д – way out

Умрёшь – начнёшь опя́ть снача́ла

умере́ть *(Perf.)* – to die; снача́ла – from the beginning

И повтори́тся всё, как **встарь:**

повтори́ться *(Perf.)* – to repeat; встарь – in old times

Ночь, ледяна́я рябь кана́ла,

ледяно́й – icy; рябь *(f., sg.)* – ripples; кана́л – canal

Апте́ка, у́лица, фона́рь.

Лексика и грамматика

1. Find the root and the prefix in "бессмы́сленный" and write down their meanings in English.

_____

Make up a sentence with this word._____

2. Find the root in "повтори́ться" and write down its meaning in English._____

Can you think of any other words with the same root?_____

_____

Make up a sentence with this word._____

3. Начнёшь – снача́ла share a common root. Find the root and write down its meaning in

English. _____. Make up two sentences with these words._____

_____

_____

4. Find the root in "исхо́д" and write down its meaning in English. Can you think of any other

words with the same root? _____

Can you guess what "безысхо́дный" means? _____

Вопросы для обсуждения

1. In your opinion, what is the poem about?

2. How do you undertand the lines "Умрёшь – начнёшь опя́ть снача́ла / И повтори́тся всё, как встарь"?

3. Can you draw a picture of the city landscape that Blok is describing? Can you guess what city is portrayed in the poem?

Гроза́ прошла́, и ве́тка бе́лых роз . . .** (1899)

Гроза́ прошла́, и **ве́тка** бе́лых роз	гроза́ – thunderstorm; ве́тка – branch
В окно́ мне **ды́шит арома́том** . . .	дыша́ть (+ *Intr.; Impf.*) – to breathe; арома́т – aroma
Ещё **трава́ полна́ прозра́чных слёз,**	трава́ – grass; полна́ – full; прозра́чный – transparent; слёзы – tears
И **гром вдали́ греми́т раска́том.**	гром – thunder; вдали́ – in the distance; греме́ть *(Impf.)* – to thunder; раска́т – peal

Лексика и грамматика

1. Find the prefix and the root in "прошла́" and give their meanings in English._____

_____. Can you think of any other words with the same root?_____

_____

Make up a sentence with this verb. _____

Can you guess what "про́шлое" means? _____. Make up a sentence

with this word. _____

2. По́лон – полна́ – полно́ – полны́ means "full of." In the poem Blok uses the the term for a metaphor about raindrops: "трава́ полна́ прозра́чных слёз." Be a poet and make up a sentence with "по́лон/полна́." Remember that you need to maintain gender agreement between the subject and the short adjective and to use the Genitive case after "по́лон."_____

_____

3. How many simple sentences does the poem contain? Write them down here._____

_____

_____

Вопросы для обсуждения

1. What is the mood of the poem?

2. What time of the year is described in the poem?

3. Compare this poem with Tyutchev's "Люблю́ грозу́ в нача́ле ма́я" above. What are their similarities and differences?

4. What is your favorite season and why?

Ве́тер принёс издалёка . . . ** (1901)

Ве́тер принёс издалёка	ве́тер – wind; принести́ *(Perf.)* – to bring; издалёка *(poet.)* – from afar; contemporary form: издалека́
Пе́сни весе́нней **намёк,**	пе́сня – song; намёк – hint
Где-то **светло́ и глубо́ко**	светло́ – lightly; глубо́ко – deeply
Не́ба откры́лся клочо́к.	не́бо – sky; откры́ться *(Perf.)* – to open; клоч/о́/к – patch

В э́той **бездо́нной лазу́ри,**   бездо́нный – bottomless; лазу́рь *(f.)* – azure

В **су́мерках** бли́зкой весны́   су́мерки *(pl.)* – twilight

Пла́кали зи́мние **бу́ри,**   пла́кать *(Impf.)* – to cry; бу́ря – storm

Ре́яли звёздные сны.   ре́ять *(Impf.)* – to soar; звёздный – starry; с/о/н – dream

Ро́бко, темно́ и глубо́ко   ро́бко – timidly; темно́ – darkly

Пла́кали **стру́ны** мои́.   стру́ны – strings

Ве́тер принёс издалёка

Зву́чные пе́сни твои́.   зву́чный – *here:* sonorous

Лексика и грамматика

1. Find the prefix and the root in "принёс" and write down their meanings in English._____

_____. Can you think of any other words with the same root?_____

_____

Make up a sentence with this verb. _____

2. Find the prefix and the root in "издалёка" and write down their meanings in

English._____. Can you think of any other words with the same

root?_____

3. Find all the adverbs in the poem (5) and list them here._____

_____

Make up two sentences with any of these adverbs._____

1. What is the poem about?

2. What time of year is described in the poem?

3. How does the spring awakening compare to the awakening of the soul of the poet?

Де́вушка пе́ла в церко́вном хо́ре . . . ** (1905)

Де́вушка пе́ла в **церко́вном хо́ре**	церко́вный – church; хо́р – choir
О всех **уста́лых в чужо́м краю́**,	уста́лый – tired; чужо́й – foreign; край – *here:* land
О всех **корабля́х, уше́дших** в мо́ре,	кора́бль – ship; уше́дший – gone away
О всех, **забы́вших ра́дость** свою́.	забы́вший – forgotten; ра́дость *(f.)* – joy
Так пел её **го́лос, летя́щий в ку́пол**,	го́лос – voice; летя́щий – flying; ку́пол – cupola
И **луч сия́л** на бе́лом **плече́**,	луч – ray; сия́ть *(Impf.)* – to shine; плечо́ – shoulder
И ка́ждый из **мра́ка** смотре́л и слу́шал,	мра́к *(sg.)* – darkness
Как бе́лое пла́тье пе́ло в луче́.	
И всем **каза́лось**, что ра́дость бу́дет,	каза́ться (+ *D.*) – to seem
Что в **ти́хой за́води** все корабли́,	ти́хая за́водь *(f.)* – peaceful harbor
Что на **чужби́не** уста́лые лю́ди	чужби́на – foreign land
Све́тлую жизнь себе́ **обрели́**.	све́тлый – light; here: happy; обрести́ – to find

И голос был **сладок**, и луч был **тонок**,   слад/о/к – sweet; тон/о/к – fine

И только высоко, у **царских врат**,   высоко – high; царский – tsar; врата *(pl.)* – gates

Причастный тайнам, – плакал ребёнок   причастный – privy; тайна – mystery

О том, что никто не придёт **назад**.   назад – back

Лексика и грамматика

1. Find all the participles (3) in the poem, write down their tense and type, and list the infinitives from which they are formed._____

_____

Make up two sentences with any of these participles._____

_____

2. Чужой – чужбина share a common root. Find the root and write down its meaning in English.

_____. Make up a sentence with any of these words._____

3. Reread the third stanza: "И всем казалось, что радость будет. . . ." Be a poet and finish the following sentence: Всем казалось, что_____

_____

Вопросы для обсуждения

1. What is the mood of the poem?

2. What is the girl singing about?

3. How do the listeners react?

4. Who is the child mentioned in the last stanza? How do you understand the end of the poem?

Грустя́ и пла́ча, и смея́сь . . . ** (1908)

Грустя́ и пла́ча и смея́сь,	грустя́ – being sad; пла́ча – crying; смея́сь – laughing
Звеня́т ручьи́ мои́х стихо́в	звене́ть *(Impf.)* – to ring; руч/е́/й – stream
У **ног** твои́х,	нога́ – foot
И ка́ждый **стих**	стих – verse
Бежи́т, **плетёт** живу́ю **вязь,**	плести́ *(Impf.)* – to weave; вязь *(f.)* – *here:* ornament
Свои́х не зна́я **берего́в**.	бе́рег – shore
Но **сквозь хруста́льные струи́**	сквозь – through; хруста́льный – crystal; струя́ – stream
Ты далека́ мне, как была́ . . .	
Пою́т и пла́чут хрустали́ . . .	петь *(Impf.)* – to sing; пла́кать *(Impf.)* – to cry; хруста́ль – crystal
Как мне **созда́ть черты́** твои,	созда́ть *(Perf.)* – to create; черта́ – feature
Чтоб ты прийти́ ко мне могла́	чтоб *(poet.)* – чтобы – in order to
Из **очаро́ванной да́ли**?	очаро́ванный – enchanted; даль *(f.)* – distance

Лексика и грамматика

1. Далека́ – даль share a common root. Find the root and write down its meaning in English.

_____. Do you know any other words with the same root?

146

_____. Make up a sentence with any of these words.

_____

2. Find all the gerunds in the poem (4) and list the verbs from which they are formed._____

_____

Make up two sentences with any of these gerunds. _____

_____

3. Find the subject in the first sentence, "Грустя́ и пла́ча и смея́сь, / звеня́т ручьи́ мои́х

стихо́в." _____

4. Reread the last sentence of the poem: "Как мне созда́ть черты́ твои́ . . . ?" The construction

Dative + infinitive has the modal meaning of "How can I?" Make up a question with this

construction: Как мне _____?

Вопросы для обсуждения

1. Whom does the poet address?

2. How do you understand the lines "Как мне созда́ть черты́ твои́"?

3. What imagery is used in the poem? How can you tell that this poem belongs to the Symbolist movement?

О до́блестях, о по́двигах, о сла́ве . . . ** (1908)

This poem is addressed to Blok's wife, Lyubov Mendeleeva, the daughter of the famous chemist Dmitry Mendeleev, whose name is associated with the creation of the *Table of Elements*. It reflects the episode in Blok's life when Lyubov fell in love with a friend of Blok's, another Symbolist poet, Andrei Bely, and thought of leaving Blok.

О **доблестях**, о **подвигах**, о **славе**	доблесть *(f.)* – valor; подвиг – exploit; слава – glory
Я забывал на **горестной земле**,	горестный – sorrowful; земля – earth
Когда твоё лицо в **простой оправе**	простой – simple; оправа – frame
Передо мной **сияло** на столе.	сиять *(Impf.)* – to shine
Но час **настал**, и ты ушла из дому.	настать *(Perf.)* – to come
Я **бросил** в ночь **заветное кольцо**.	бросить *(Perf.)* – to throw; заветный – cherished; кольцо – ring
Ты отдала свою **судьбу** другому,	судьба – destiny
И я забыл прекрасное лицо.	
Летели дни, **крутясь проклятым роем** . . .	крутясь – swirling; проклятый – cursed; рой – swarm
Вино и **страсть терзали** жизнь мою . . .	страсть – passion; терзать *(Impf.)* – to torment
И вспомнил я тебя **пред аналоем**,	пред *(poet.)* – in front of; аналой – altar
И **звал** тебя, как **молодость** свою . . .	звать *(Impf.)* – to call; молодость *(f.)* – youth
Я звал тебя, но ты не **оглянулась**,	оглянуться *(Perf.)* – to look back
Я **слёзы лил**, но ты не **снизошла**.	слёзы – tears; лить *(Impf.)* – to weep; снизойти *(Perf.)* – to condescend
Ты в **синий плащ печально завернулась**,	синий – dark blue; плащ – cloak; печально – sadly; завернуться *(Perf.)* – to wrap oneself

В **сыру́ю** ночь ты и́з дому ушла́.

сыро́й – damp

Не зна́ю, где **прию́т** свое́й **гордыне**

прию́т – to shelter; гордыня – pride

Ты, ми́лая, ты, **не́жная**, нашла́ . . .

не́жный – tender

Я **кре́пко** сплю, **мне сни́тся** плащ твой си́ний,

кре́пко – *here:* soundly, мне сни́тся – I dream

В кото́ром ты в сыру́ю ночь ушла́ . . .

Уж не мечта́ть о не́жности, о сла́ве,

Уж не – уже́ не – no longer

Всё **минова́лось,** мо́лодость прошла́!

минова́ться *(Perf., arch.)* – to pass

Твоё лицо́ в его́ просто́й опра́ве

Свое́й руко́й **убра́л** я со стола́.

убра́ть *(Perf.)* – to remove

Лексика и грамматика

1. Го́рестный – го́ре – горева́ть – го́рький share a common root. Find the root and write down its meaning in English. _____. Make up two sentences with these words.

_____

_____

2. Не́жная – не́жность share a common root. Find the root and write down its meaning in English. _____. Make up a sentence with any of these words.

_____

3. Find all the third-declension nouns (6)._____

_____

Make up three sentences with these nouns._____

_____

_____

4. Be a poet and finish the following sentence: Я крéпко сплю, мне снúтся_____

_____

Вопросы для обсуждения

1. What is the mood of the poem?

2. What happened in the relationship between the lyric hero and his beloved?

3. How do you understand the lines "И звал тебя, как мóлодость свою"?

4. How did his feelings change afterward?

Оний читáют стихú ** (1908)

This poem is from the cycle *Снéжная мáска,* dedicated to Natalya Vólokhova. In the winter of 1908–1909 Blok fell in love with Volokhova and wrote her many passionate poems, which later formed two poetic cycles.

Смотрú: я **спýтал** все **странúцы**,	спýтать *(Perf.)* – to mix up; странúца – page
Покá глазá твоú **цвелú**.	покá – while; глазá – eyes; цвестú *(Impf.)* – to bloom
Большúе крýлья снéжной птúцы	крýлья – wings; снéжный – snowy; птúца – bird
Мой **ум метéлью замелú**.	ум – mind; метéль *(f.)* – blizzard; заместú *(Perf.)* – *here:* to cover
Как **стрáнны** бы́ли **рéчи мáски!**	стрáнный – strange; рéчь *(f.)* – speech, here: words; мáска – mask
Поня́тны ли тебé? – **Бог весть!**	Бог весть *(idiom.)* – God knows!

Ты **твёрдо** зна́ешь: в кни́гах – **ска́зки**,	твёрдо – firmly; ска́зка – fairy tale
А в жи́зни – **то́лько про́за** есть.	то́лько – only; про́за – prose
Но для меня́ **нераздели́мы**	нераздели́мы – inseparable
С тобо́ю – ночь, и **мгла** реки́,	мгла – darkness
И **застыва́ющие ды́мы**,	застыва́ющий – cooling; дым – smoke
И **рифм** весёлых **ого́ньки**.	ри́фма – rhyme; огон/ё/к – light
Не будь и ты со мно́ю **стро́гой**	стро́гий – strict
И ма́ской не **дразни́** меня́,	дразни́ть *(Impf.)* – to tease
И в тёмной па́мяти не **тро́гай**	тёмный – dark; па́мять *(f.)* – memory; тро́гать *(Impf.)* – to touch
Ино́го – стра́шного – огня́.	ино́й – different; стра́шный – frightening; ог/о́/нь – fire

Лексика и грамматика

1. Сне́жная – снег – снежи́нка share a common root. Find the root and write down its **meaning** in English. _____. Make up a sentence with any of these words.

_____

2. "Огон/ё/к" is formed from "ог/о́/нь" (fire) with the diminitive suffix "–ок." Can **you think of** any other diminutive nouns? _____

3. Find all the imperatives in the poem (4) and list them here. _____

_____

Make up three sentences with the imperative construction._____

Вопросы для обсуждения

1. What is the poem about?

2. To whom is the poet speaking?

3. How do you understand the beloved's views on life and literature as expressed in the second stanza: "ты твёрдо зна́ешь – в кни́гах ска́зки, / а в жи́зни то́лько про́за есть"? Do you agree or disagree?

4. How does the lyric hero respond to that?

5. Do you like the poem? Why?

Весе́нний день прошёл без де́ла . . . ** (1909)

Весе́нний день прошёл **без де́ла**	без де́ла *(idiom.)* – without [my having] anything to do
У **неумы́того** окна́;	неумы́тый – unwashed
Скуча́ла за **стено́й** и пе́ла,	скуча́ть *(Impf.)* – to be bored; стена – wall
Как **пти́ца пле́нная**, жена́.	пти́ца – bird; пле́нный – captive
Я, не спеша́, собра́л бесстра́стно	не спеша́ – not hurrying; собра́ть *(Perf.)* – to gather; бесстра́стно – dispassionately
Воспомина́нья и дела́;	воспомина́нье – memory
И стало **беспоща́дно я́сно**:	беспоща́дно – ruthlessly; я́сно – clear
Жизнь **прошуме́ла** и ушла́.	прошуме́ть *(Perf.)* – lit. to make noise; *here:* to clatter
Ещё **верну́тся мы́сли, спо́ры**,	верну́ться *(Perf.)* – to return; мы́сль *(f.)* – thought; спор – argument

Но бу́дет **ску́чно и темно́**;   ску́чно – boring; темно́ – dark

К чему́ спуска́ть на о́кнах **што́ры**? К чему́ – *here:* what for? спуска́ть *(Perf.)* – to lower; што́ры –

                                             drapes

День **догоре́л** в душе́ **давно́**.   догоре́ть *(Perf.)* – to burn out; давно́ – a long time ago

Лексика и грамматика

1. Скуча́ть – ску́чно – ску́ка share a common root. Find the root and write down its meaning in

English. _____. Make up a sentence with any of these words.

_____

2. Find the prefix and the root in "прошуме́л" and write down their meanings in

English._____. Can you think of any other words with the same

root?_____

3. Find the prefix and the root in "бесстра́стно" and write down their meanings in English.

_____. Do you know any other words with the same root?

_____

4. Find the prefix and the root in "воспомина́нье" and write down their meanings in English.

_____. Can you think of any other words with the same root?

_____

Make up a sentence with this word._____

Вопросы для обсуждения

1. What is the mood of the poem?

2. How is the metaphor of the day ending outside and the "day" in the soul of the poet played out in the poem? Find specific examples in the text.

3. Compare this poem to Lermontov's "И скучно, и грустно . . ." above. What do they have in common and how are they different? Which poem do you like better and why?

А́нне Ахма́товой ** (1913)

"Красота́ страшна́" – Вам ска́жут, –	красота́ – beauty; страшна́ – frightening
Вы наки́нете лени́во	наки́нуть (*Perf.*) – *here:* to drape; лени́во – lazily
Шаль испа́нскую на пле́чи,	шаль (*f.*) – shawl; пле́чи – shoulders
Кра́сный ро́зан – в волоса́х.	ро́зан (*poet.*) – rose; во́лосы – hair
"Красота́ проста́" – Вам ска́жут, –	проста́ – simple
Пёстрой ша́лью неуме́ло	пёстрый – motley; неуме́ло – awkwardly
Вы укро́ете ребёнка,	укры́ть (*Perf.*) – to cover
Кра́сный ро́зан – на полу́.	
Но, рассе́янно внима́я	рассе́янно – absently; внима́я (*arch.*) – listening
Всем слова́м, круго́м звуча́щим,	круго́м – around; звуча́щий – sounding
Вы заду́маетесь гру́стно	заду́маться (*Perf.*) – to fall to thinking
И тверди́те про себя́:	тверди́ть (*Impf.*) – to repeat; про себя́ – to yourself
"Не страшна́ и не проста́ я;	

Я не так страшна́, **чтоб** про́сто   чтоб – чтобы – in order to

Убива́ть, не так проста́ я,   убива́ть *(Impf.)* – to kill

Чтоб не знать, как жизнь страшна́."

Ле́ксика и грамма́тика

1. Find the prefix and the root in "заду́маться" and write down their meanings in

English._____. Can you think of any other words

with the same root? _____

Make up a sentence with this word._____

2. Find the root in "тверди́ть" and write down its meaning in English._____

_____. Can you think of any other words with the same root?_____

_____

Make up a sentence with any of these words._____

3. What tense and aspect are used in the first and second stanzas?_____

4. Reread the ending of the poem: "я не так страшна́, чтоб про́сто / убива́ть, и не так проста́

я, / чтоб не знать, как жизнь страшна́." Translate it into English. _____

_____

Вопро́сы для обсужде́ния:

1. What is the poem about?

2. What images representing two types of beauty does the poet create? How do you understand
his juxtaposition?

3. How do you understand the final stanza?

О, я хочу́ безу́мно жить . . . ** (1914)

О, я хочу́ **безу́мно** жить:	безу́мно – madly
Всё **су́щее** – **увекове́чить**,	су́щее – existing; увекове́чить *(Perf.)* – to immortalize
Безли́чное – **вочелове́чить**,	безли́чное – faceless; вочелове́чить *(poet., Perf.)* – to humanize
Несбы́вшееся – **воплоти́ть!**	несбы́вшееся – *here:* what did not happen; воплоти́ть *(Perf.)* – to make materialize
Пусть **ду́шит** жи́зни сон **тяжёлый**,	души́ть *(Impf.)* – to strangle; тяжёлый – heavy
Пусть **задыха́юсь** в э́том сне, –	задыха́ться *(Impf.)* – to suffocate
Быть мо́жет, **ю́ноша** весёлый	ю́ноша – young man
В **гряду́щем** ска́жет обо мне:	гряду́щее – future
Прости́м угрю́мство – ра́зве э́то	прости́ть *(Perf.)* – to forgive; угрю́мство – gloom; ра́зве – is it really
Сокры́тый дви́гатель его́?	сокры́тый – hidden; дви́гатель – *here:* drive
*Он **весь** – **дитя́ добра́ и све́та**,*	весь – the whole; дитя́ – child; добро́ – good; свет – light
*Он весь – **свободы торжество́**!*	свобо́да – freedom; торжество́ – triumph

156

Лексика и грамматика

1. Find the prefix and the root in "увеко́вечить" and write down their meanings in English.

_____. Can you think of any other words with the same root?

_____

Make up a sentence with this verb. _____

2. Find the prefix and the root in "безли́чное" and write down their meanings in English._____

_____. Can you think of any other words with the same root?_____

_____

3. Find the prefix and the root in "несбы́вшееся" and write down their meanings in English.

_____. Can you think of any other words with the same

root? _____

Can you guess what "сбы́вшееся" means? _____

Make up a sentence with any of these words._____

4. In the poem we read, "Он весь – дитя́ добра́ и све́та." Весь – вся – всё – все in this context means "the whole." Be a poet and finish the following sentence: Он весь / Она вся_____

_____

Вопросы для обсуждения

1. What does the poem assert?

2. How do you understand the lines in the first stanza: "Всё су́щее – увеко́вечить, / безли́чное – очелове́чить, / несбы́вшееся – воплоти́ть!"?

3. How does the poet want to be viewed by posterity?

4. Compare this poem to Pushkin's "Я па́мятник себе́ воздви́г нерукотво́рный . . ." above.

Мари́на Ива́новна Цвета́ева (1892–1941)

Marina Tsvetaeva was one of the great poets of the Silver Age. Her father was a philologist, a professor at Moscow University, and the founder of the Pushkin Museum of Fine Arts in Moscow, to the creation of which he dedicated twenty-five years of his life. Her mother was a talented pianist who was not able to pursue a professional career because of opposition from her own father, who thought that it was not a suitable occupation for a gentlewoman. Her passion for music found its outlet in the home teaching of her daughters. The elder, Marina, showed great promise early on, and it was thought that she would become a professional pianist and fulfill the aspirations of her mother. But Marina was always more interested in literature, and she abandoned her piano studies when her mother died of tuberculosis in 1906, when Tsvetaeva was only fourteen years old. Some of the best known and most beloved of Tsvetaeva's prose works were written about her parents—"Оте́ц и его музе́й" (My Father and His Museum), "Ска́зка ма́тери" (Mother's Tale), and "Мать и му́зыка" (My Mother and Music).

Tsvetaeva published her first collection of poems, *Вечéрний альбóм* (*The Evening Album*), in 1910; five hundred copies were printed with her own money, and immediately gained recognition in Moscow literary circles. She became friends with many prominent figures of the Silver Age, among them Valery Bryusov, Maximilian Voloshin, Osip Mandelshtam, and later Boris Pasternak and Andrei Bely. In 1912 she married Sergei Efron, and they had two daughters. With the beginning of World War I, Efron joined the army as a male nurse; then after the revolution of 1917 he fought in the White Army. Tsvetaeva continued to live in Moscow in great poverty in a country ravaged by revolution and civil war, not knowing the fate of her husband. In the winter of 1919–1920 Tsvetaeva had to put her children in an orphanage, believing that there they would be fed better and survive the harsh winter. When Tsvetaeva visited them there, she saw that her older daughter, Ariadna, was ill, and she took her home, but in February 1920 she heard that her younger daughter, Irina, had died of hunger in the orphanage. Finally, in 1921 Tsvetaeva learned that her husband was alive in Prague, and she and Ariadna went there to join him. They remained in Prague until November 1925, and their third child, Georgy, was born there in February of that year.

The years in Prague were very productive for Tsvetaeva. She continued to write poetry and prose, contributed to the emigré literary journals, and published her two long poems, *Poem of the Hill (Поэма Горы)* and *Poem of the End (Поэма Концá)*. While in Prague, she also wrote two folk poems, "*Tsar-Maiden*" (*Царь-девúца*), which she later translated into French, and "*The Swain*" (*Мóлодец*). From Russian folk tales Tsvetaeva turned to German folklore and began a long poem based on the legend of the Pied Piper of Hamelin, *Крысолóв* (*Pied Piper*). Her intense epistolary friendship with Boris Pasternak also began in this period. Pasternak highly praised Tsvetaeva's talent and sensed a deep affinity between his own poetry and hers. Similarly, she felt that Pasternak's poetic worldview was very close to her own, and over the years they continued to support each other and exchange letters and poems. Later Pasternak wrote to Ariadna: "В течéние нéскольких лет меня́ держáло в постоя́нной счастли́вой припóднятости всё, что писáла тогдá твоя мáма, звóнкий, восхищáющий резонáнс ее рву́щегося вперёд, безогля́дного одухотворéния" (for several years I was in a state of constant elation with everything that your mother wrote, with her admirable resonance of forward-gushing, reckless spiritualization) (cited in В. Швейцер, "Быт и бытие Марины Цветаевой"; Moscow, СП Интерпринт, 1992, p. 359).

Knowing that Tsvetaeva revered the great poet Rainer Maria Rilke and deeply admired his work, in 1926 Pasternak, who knew Rilke personally, wrote to Rilke telling him about Tsvetaeva's poetry and sent him some of her poems. Rilke knew enough Russian to be able to read her poems, and a correspondence between him and Tsvetaeva began. This poetic exchange was interrupted by Rilke's death in December 1926. When Tsvetaeva learned about his passing, she wrote a poem, "Новогóднее" (New Year's Greetings), as a letter to her departed friend, as if continuing their correspondence: "Что мне дéлать в новогóднем шу́ме / С этой вну́треннею ри́фмой: Рáйнер – у́мер." She also wrote an essay, "Твоя смерть" (Your Death).

After moving to Paris, the family spent many years in very difficult financial circumstances. Tsvetaeva was the main breadwinner, and she supported her family by a small stipend from the

Czech authorities, given to her as a writer, and by an irregular income from publications in the emigré journals, poetry recitations, and translations. Sergei Efron's main interests remained in politics. Over the years his political views had undergone a dramatic change. In Paris he formed Союз Возвращéния (the Union of the Return) for those who wanted to return to Russia; later it became known that he was serving as a secret agent for a Soviet intelligence service. In 1937 Ariadna returned to Moscow, and then Sergei Efron, whose indentity as a secret agent had been discovered in France, returned as well. Marina did not want to go back to Russia but could not be separated from her family, so she reluctantly followed Efron in the summer of 1939. That same year he was arrested, and he was shot in August 1941. Ariadna was also arrested and sentenced to many years of exile and was rehabilitated only in 1955. Tsvetaeva was not able to publish any of her work or earn any money. She hanged herself on August 31, 1941, in the city of Yelabuga, where she had been evacuated, because Nazi troops were rapidly advancing on Moscow. In her last note to her son Georgy she wrote: "Пойми, что я бóльше не моглá жить" (Please understand that I could not go on living any more).

Крáсною кúстью . . . * (1916)

Крáсною кúстью	кúсть *(f.)* – cluster
Рябúна зажглáсь.	рябúна – ash berry; зажéчься *(Perf.)* – to light up
Пáдали лúстья.	пáдать – to fall; лúстья – leaves
Я родилáсь.	родúться *(Perf.)* – to be born
Спóрили сóтни	спóрить *(Impf.)* – to argue; сóтня – hundred

Колоколо́в.	ко́локол – bell,
День был **суббо́тний**:	суббо́тний *(adj.)* – *cf.* суббо́та
Иоа́нн Богосло́в.	St. John the Evangelist

Мне и **доны́не**	доны́не – until now
Хо́чется грызть	хо́чется (+ *D.*) – to feel like; грызть *(Impf.)* – to nibble
Жа́ркой ряби́ны	жа́ркий – hot
Го́рькую кисть.	го́рький – bitter

Лексика и грамматика

1. Find all the verbs in the past tense (5) and identify their aspect._____

_____

2. List all the adjectives in the poem (4)._____

_____. Make up two sentences with these words.

_____

_____

3. Жа́ркий – пожа́р – жара́ share a common root. Find the root and write down its meaning in

English. _____. Make up two sentences with these words.

_____

_____

4. Finish the following sentence: Мне хо́чется_____

1. What is the poem about?

2. How does the poet describe the day when she was born?

3. How do you understand the line "Спо́рили со́тни колоколо́в"?

4. What is the tone of the poem? Is it happy or sad?

Мои́м стиха́м, напи́санным так ра́но . . . ** (1913)

Мои́м **стиха́м, напи́санным** так ра́но,	стихи́ – poems; напи́санный – written
Что и не зна́ла я, что я – поэ́т,	
Сорва́вшимся, как **бры́зги** из фонта́на,	сорва́вшийся – broken loose; бры́зги *(pl.)* – splashes
Как **и́скры** из **раке́т,**	и́скра – spark; раке́та – rocket
Ворва́вшимся, как ма́ленькие **че́рти,**	ворва́вшийся – having burst into; чёрт – devil
В **святи́лище,** где сон и **фимиа́м,**	святи́лище – sanctuary; фимиа́м – frankincense
Мои́м стиха́м о **ю́ности** и **сме́рти,**	ю́ность *(f.)* – youth; сме́рть *(f.)* – death
– **Нечи́танным** стиха́м!	нечи́танный – unread
Разбро́санным в **пыли́** по магази́нам,	разбро́санный – scattered; пыль *(f.)* – dust
Где их никто́ не брал и не берёт,	
Мои́м стиха́м, как **драгоце́нным** ви́нам,	драгоце́нный – precious
Наста́нет свой черёд.	(Their) time will come

164

Лексика и грамматика

1. Find all the participles in the poem (5); write down their meanings in English, indicating whether they are passive or active, and list the verbs from which the participles are formed.

_____

_____

2. "Драгоце́нный" has two roots. Find the roots and write down their meanings in English.

_____. Make up a sentence with this word.

_____

3. List all the nouns of the third declension (3). _____

Make up sentences with each of these words._____

_____

_____

4. Syntactically the poem consists of one long sentence. Can you identify the main sentence?

_____

Вопросы для обсуждения

1. What is the poem about?

2. What is the poet's prediction about her work?

3. Do your own research on Marina Tsvetaeva and find out if her prediction came true.

Идёшь, на меня похо́жий . . . ** (1913)

Идёшь, на меня́ **похо́жий**,	похо́жий – similar, alike
Глаза́ **устремля́я вниз**.	устремля́ть *(Impf.)* – to direct; вниз – down
Я их **опуска́ла** – то́же!	опуска́ть *(Impf.)* – to lower
Прохо́жий, остановись!	прохо́жий – passerby; останови́ться *(Perf.)* – to stop
Прочти́ – **слепоты́ кури́ной**	кури́ная слепота́ – *here:* buttercup
И **ма́ков набра́в буке́т** –	мак – poppy; набра́ть *(Perf.)* – *here:* to gather; буке́т – bouquet
Что зва́ли меня́ Мари́ной	
И ско́лько мне бы́ло лет.	
Не ду́май, что здесь – **моги́ла**,	моги́ла – grave
Что я **появлю́сь, грозя́** . . .	появи́ться *(Perf.)* – to appear; грози́ть *(Impf.)* – to threaten
Я **сли́шком** сама́ люби́ла	сли́шком – too much
Смея́ться, когда́ нельзя́!	
И **кровь прилива́ла к ко́же**,	кровь *(f.)* – blood; прилива́ть – *here:* to flush; ко́жа – skin
И **ку́дри** мой **вили́сь** . . .	ку́дри – locks, ви́ться *(Impf.)* – *here:* to curl
Я то́же была́, прохо́жий!	
Прохо́жий, остановись!	
Сорви́ себе **сте́бель ди́кий**	сорва́ть *(Perf.)* – to pick; сте́бель – stem; ди́кий – wild

И **я́году** ему́ **вслед:**	я́года – berry; вслед – to follow
Кладби́щенской земляни́ки	кладби́щенский – cemeterial; земляни́ка *(sg.)* – wild strawberry
Крупне́е и **сла́ще** нет.	крупне́е *(comp.* of кру́пный) – large; сла́ще – (comp. of сла́дкий) – sweet
Но то́лько не стой **угрю́мо,**	угрю́мо – gloomy
Главу́ **опусти́в** на **грудь.**	опусти́ть *(Perf.)* – to lower; грудь *(f.)* – chest
Легко́ обо мне поду́май,	
Легко́ обо мне забу́дь.	
Как **луч** тебя́ **освеща́ет!**	луч – ray; освеща́ть *(Impf.)* – to light
Ты весь в **золото́й пыли́** . . .	золото́й – golden; пыль *(f.)* – dust
– И пусть тебя́ не **смуща́ет**	смуща́ть *(Impf.) – here:* to disturb
Мой го́лос **из-под земли́.**	из-под – from under; земля́ – *here:* ground

Лексика и грамматика

1. "Прохо́жий" means passerby. Find the prefix and the root and write down their meanings in English. _____. Make up a sentence with this word.

_____

2. Освеща́ть – свет – све́тлый share a common root. Find the root and write down its meaning in English. _____. Make up two sentences with these words.

_____

_____

3. Find all the imperatives in the poem (8) and list them and the infinitives from which they are formed. _____

_____

Вопросы для обсуждения

1. What is the main theme of the poem?

2. Where is the poem taking place?

3. How does the poet want to be remembered?

4. What is the overall mood of the poem? Is it happy or sad?

Стихи́ расту́т, как звёзды и как ро́зы . . . ** (1918)

Стихи́ **расту́т**, как **звёзды** и как ро́зы,	расти́ *(Perf.)* – to grow; звезда́ – star
Как красота́ – **нену́жная** в семье́.	нену́жный – unneccessary
А на **венцы́** и на **апофео́зы** –	вен/е́/ц – wreath; апофео́з – apotheosis
Оди́н отве́т: – Отку́да мне **сие́**?	сие́ *(arch.)* – это
Мы спим – и вот, сквозь **ка́менные пли́ты**,	сквозь – through; ка́менная плита́ – tombstone
Небе́сный гость в четы́ре **лепестка́**.	небе́сный – celestial; лепест/о́/к – petal
О мир, пойми́! **Певцо́м – во сне** – откры́ты	пев/е́/ц – *here:* poet; во сне – in a dream
Зако́н звезды́ и фо́рмулы **цветка́**.	зако́н – law; цвет/о́/к – flower

Лексика и грамматика

1. Певе́ц – певи́ца – петь – пе́сня share a common root. Find the root and write down its

meaning in English. _____. Make up two sentences with these words.

_____

_____

2. What is the antonym of "нену́жный"? _____. Make up two sentences with

these words. _____

_____

3. What is being described in the lines "сквозь ка́менные пли́ты / Небе́сный гость в четы́ре

лепестка́"? _____

Вопросы для обсуждения

1. What is the main theme of the poem?

2. What is the poet's attitude to fame?

3. According to the poet, what is the nature of inspiration?

4. Compare this poem to Pushkin's "Я па́мятник себе́ воздви́г нерукотво́рный" above.

Как пра́вая и ле́вая рука́ . . . ** (1918)

Как **пра́вая и ле́вая рука́,**	пра́вый – right; ле́вый – left; рука́ – hand
Твоя́ **душа́** мое́й душе́ **близка́.**	душа́ – soul, близка́ – close
Мы **смежены́, блаже́нно и тепло́,**	смежены́ – adjoined; блаже́нно – blissfully; тепло́ – warmly

Как пра́вое и ле́вое **крыло́**.   крыло́ – wing

Но **вихрь встаёт** – и **бе́здна пролегла́**   But the whirlwind rises – and the abyss has plunged down

От пра́вого – до ле́вого крыла́!

Лексика и грамматика

1. Find the adverbs in the poem (2) and list them here. _____

Make up a sentence with one of the adverbs. _____

2. Близка́ – бли́зкий – бли́зость – прибли́зиться share a common root. Find the root and write

down its meaning in English. _____. Make up two sentences with any of these

words._____

_____

3. Reread the first sentence. "Как" here means "as," and it introduces a comparison in Russian,

as we see in this poem. Make up a comparison with"как."_____

_____

4. Reread the last sentence. The prepositions "от + *Gen.* and до + *Gen.*" describe distance in

length—for example, "От Москвы до Петербурга 800 км." Make up a sentence with this

construction._____

Вопросы для обсуждения

1. What is the poem about?

2. What are the comparisons that Tsvetaeva uses?

3. How do you understand the metaphor of the wings?

Ятага́н? Ого́нь? …** (1924)

Ятага́н? Ого́нь?	ятага́н – yataghan, eastern sword; ого́нь – fire
Поскромне́е, – куда как гро́мко!	поскромне́е – more modestly; куда как гро́мко *(colloq.)* – far louder
Боль, знако́мая, как **глаза́м – ладо́нь,**	боль *(f.)* – pain; глаза́ – eyes; ладо́нь *(f.)* – palm
Как **губа́м –**	гу́бы – lips
И́мя **со́бственного ребёнка.**	со́бственный – one's own; ребён/о/к – child

Лексика и грамматика

1. Find the root in "знако́мая" and write down its meaning in English. _____

Can you think of any other words with the same root? List them here. _____

_____

Make up a sentence with "знако́мый/ая." _____

2. Боль – больно́й – заболе́ть – боле́знь *(f.)* share a common root. Find the root and write down

its meaning in English. _____.Make up two sentences with these words.

_____

_____

3. Reread the poem carefully. Can you guess which part of speech (noun, verb, adjective, etc.) is

completely missing from the poem?_____

Вопросы для обсуждения

1. What is the poem about?

2. What definition does the poet give to love?

3. How do you understand the lines "Поскромне́е, – куда́ как гро́мко! / Боль, знако́мая, как глаза́м – ладо́нь"?

4. Compare this poem to Blok's "Анне Ахма́товой" above ("Красота́ страшна́ – вам ска́жут . . ."). What do these poems have in common, and how are they different?

Если душа́ родила́сь крыла́той . . . ** (1918)

Е́сли душа́ родила́сь крыла́той –	душа́ – soul; крыла́тый – winged
Что́ ей хоро́мы – и что́ ей ха́ты!	Что́ ей *(idiom.)* – what would [it/they] be to her?; хоро́мы *(arch.)* – palaces; ха́ты – huts
Что **Чингис-Ха́н** ей и что – **Орда́**!	Чингис-Ха́н – Genghis Khan; Орда́ – horde
Два на **миру́** у меня́ **врага́**,	мир – *here:* world; враг – enemy
Два **близнеца́, неразры́вно-сли́тых**:	близне́ц – twin; неразры́вно-сли́тый – inseparably merged
Го́лод голо́дных – и **сы́тость** сы́тых!	го́лод – hunger; сы́тость *(f.)* – satiety

Лексика и грамматика

1. "Го́лод" means hunger. What does "голо́дный" mean? _____

2. "Сы́тость" means satiety. What does "сы́тый" mean? _____

Make up two sentences with any of these words._____

_____

3. Reread the first sentence. "Если" introduces the conditional mood. Use "если" in a sentence.

_____

Вопросы для обсуждения

1. What is the poem about?

2. Why does Tsvetaeva remember Genghis Khan?

3. How do you understand the last lines: "Два на миру́ у меня́ врага́, / два близнеца́ неразры́вно-сли́тых / Го́лод голо́дных и сы́тость сы́тых"? In your opinion, why does the poet refer to them as "близнецы́"? Do you agree or disagree with her connection?

Анна Андре́евна Ахма́това (1889–1966)

"Akhmatova" is the pen name of Anna Gorenko, who was born in Odessa in 1889. She wrote that among her ancestors there was Khan Akhmat, and hence her pen name. Akmatova's rich poetic legacy covers an unusually long chronological period (especially for a Russian poet of her generation), spanning from her early lyric love poems, written in the Silver Age, to her larger works with a social mission, such as the poem "Requiem," condemning the Stalinist terror, written in the 1930s but published in the Soviet Union only in 1987.

In 1890 Akhmatova's family moved to Tsarskoe Selo near St. Petersburg. Akhmatova studied at the Tsarskoselsky Gymnasium, where Nikolai Gumilev (who was also a student there) met her and fell in love with her. He pursued her, attempted suicide, proposed to her several times, and was finally accepted. Her first collection of poems, *Evening (Ве́чер),* was published by the Poets' Guild (Цех Поэтов) in 1912 and brought her instant acclaim for the fine psychology, lyricism, and clarity of her poetic language. Her second collection, *Rosary (Чётки)*, appeared in 1914 and solidified her fame, crowning her with such epithets as "the Soul of the Silver Age." In this period of her life Akhmatova had many close friendships with the leading poets of the Silver Age, such as Alexander Blok, Boris Pasternak, and Osip Mandelshtam.

In 1918 Gumilev and Akhmatova divorced. In 1921 Gumilev was arrested and executed. Akhmatova's and Gumilev's son, Lev, was also arrested and sent to Siberia for five years in 1938. After completing his sentence, he volunteered for and fought in World War II, but he was arrested again in 1949 and given a ten-year sentence in the labor camps. Akhmatova's long-time companion, art critic Nikolai Punin, was also arrested several times and died in the camps in 1953. Akhmatova's horrible experince as the widow and mother of victims of the Stalinist terror was reflected in her poem "Requiem."

During the Soviet period, Akhmatova's poetry was constantly censored, and in 1946 the Central Committee of the Communist Party issued a very negative assessment of her work, claiming that her poetry was irrelevant because it represented decadent bourgeois tastes and "art for art's sake." As a result, Akhmatova was expelled from the Writers' Union and was unable to publish her work. Akhmatova's membership in the Writers' Union was later reinstated. After Khrushchev's thaw in 1955 her poems began to reappear. She became a mentor and a friend to the young Petersburg poets Joseph Brodsky and Evgeny Rein, who frequented her house. She died in a sanatorium near Moscow in 1966.

Сероглазый король ** (1910)

Сла́ва тебе́, **безысхо́дная боль!**   сла́ва – glory; безысхо́дный – irreparable; боль *(f.)* – pain

У́мер вчера́ **сероглазый коро́ль.**   умере́ть *(Perf.)* – to die; сероглазый – gray-eyed; коро́ль – king

Ве́чер осе́нний был **ду́шен и ал,**   ду́шен – stuffy; ал (short form of а́лый) – scarlet

Му́ж мой, **верну́вшись, споко́йно** сказа́л: верну́вшись – having returned; споко́йно – calmly

"Зна́ешь, с **охо́ты** его́ принесли́,   охо́та – hunt

Те́ло у ста́рого **ду́ба** нашли́.   те́ло – body; ду́б – oak

Жаль короле́ву. Тако́й молодо́й! . . .   жаль – *here: it`s a pity;* короле́ва – queen

За́ ночь одну́ она́ ста́ла **седо́й.**"   за́ ночь – overnight; седо́й – gray-haired

Тру́бку свою́ на **ками́не** нашёл   тру́бка – pipe; ками́н – mantel

И на рабо́ту ночну́ю ушёл.

До́чку мою́ я сейча́с **разбужу́,**   разбуди́ть *(Perf.)* – to wake

В се́рые гла́зки её **погляжу́.**   погляде́ть *(Perf.)* – to look

А за окно́м **шелестя́т тополя́:**   шелесте́ть *(Impf.)* – to rustle; то́поль – poplar

"Нет на земле́ твоего́ короля́..."

Лексика и грамматика

1. Find two roots in "сероглáзый" and write down their meanings in English. _____

Do you know any other words with either of the same roots? List them

here._____

Make up a sentence with any of these words. _____

_____

2. Find the prefixes and the root in "безысхóдный" and write down their meanings in English.

_____

Can you think of any other words with the same root? List them here._____

_____

3. Find all the Perfective verbs in the poem (9) and list them, indicating their tenses and

meanings and their Imperfective counterparts. _____

_____

Why is the Perfective aspect used for most of the verbs in the poem?_____

4. The poem contains two diminutives. Can you find them?_____

Why are diminutives used in your opinion?_____

Вопросы для обсуждения

1. Who is telling the story in the poem?

2. What do we know about this woman?

3. What do we know about her relationship with the king? Find textual references in the poem.

4. Summarize the story in your own words.

Па́мять о со́лнце . . . ** (1911)

Па́мять о **со́лнце** в **се́рдце слабе́ет.**	па́мять *(f.)* – memory; со́лнце – sun; се́рдце – heart; слабе́ть *(Impf.)* – to weaken
Желте́й трава́.	желте́й –yellower; трава́ – grass
Ве́тер снежи́нками ра́нними **ве́ет**	ве́тер – wind; снежи́нка – snowflake; ве́ять *(Impf.)* – to blow
Едва́ –едва́.	едва́ – barely
В **у́зких кана́лах** уже́ не **струи́тся** –	узкий – narrow; кана́л – canal; струи́ться *(Impf.)* – to flow
Сты́нет вода́.	сты́нуть *(Impf.)* – *here:* to freeze
Здесь никогда́ ничего́ не случи́тся, –	
О, никогда́!	
И́ва на не́бе **пусто́м распласта́ла**	и́ва – willow; пусто́й – empty; распласта́ть *(Perf.)* – to spread
Ве́ер сквозно́й.	ве́ер – fan; сквозно́й – transparent
Мо́жет быть, лу́чше, что я не ста́ла	
Ва́шей жено́й.	
Па́мять о со́лнце в се́рдце слабе́ет.	
Что́ это? **Тьма?**	тьма – darkness
Мо́жет быть! . . . **За́ ночь** прийти́ **успе́ет**	за́ ночь – overnight; успе́ть *(Perf.)* – to manage
Зима́.	

Ле́ксика и грамма́тика

1. Слабе́ет – сла́бый – сла́бость *(f.)* share a common root. Find the root and write down its meaning in English. _____.

Make up a sentence with any of these words.

_____

2. Память *(f.)* – помнить – воспоминание share a common root. Find the root and write down

its meaning in English. _____. Make up two sentences with these words.

_____

_____

3. Reread the last sentence. "Успеть" means to manage to do something within the constraints of

time. For example, Я успел купить продукты до того, как магазин закрылся. Они успели на

поезд. Make up a sentence with успеть._____

_____

Вопросы для обсуждения

1. What is the mood of the landscape?

2. What time of year does Akhmatova describe?

3. How does it correspond to the emotional state of the poet?

Вечером ** (1913)

Звенела музыка в саду́	звене́ть *(Impf.)* – *here:* to sound
Таки́м **невырази́мым го́рем.**	невырази́мый – inexpressible; го́ре – grief
Свежо́ и о́стро па́хли мо́рем	свежо́ – freshly; о́стро – sharply; па́хнуть *(Impf. + Instr.)* – to smell; мо́ре – sea
На **блю́де у́стрицы** во льду́.	блю́до – platter; у́стрица – oyster

Он мне сказа́л: "Я ве́рный друг!"	ве́рный – loyal
И моего́ косну́лся пла́тья.	косну́ться *(Perf. + Gen.)* – to touch
Как не похо́жи на объя́тья	объя́тье – embrace
Прикоснове́нья э́тих рук.	прикоснове́нье – touch
Так гла́дят ко́шек или птиц,	гла́дить *(Impf.)* – to stroke; пти́ца – bird
Так на нае́здниц смо́трят стро́йных . . .	нае́здница – equestrienne; стро́йный – slender
Лишь смех в глаза́х его́ споко́йных	лишь – only; смех – laughter
Под лёгким зо́лотом ресни́ц.	зо́лото – gold; ресни́ца – lash
А ско́рбных скри́пок голоса́	ско́рбный – mournful; скри́пка – violin; го́лос – voice
Пою́т за сте́лющимся ды́мом:	сте́лющийся – *here:* trailing, дым – smoke
"Благослови́ же небеса́ –	благослови́ть *(Perf.)* – to bless; же – emphatic particle;
	небеса́ – heaven
Ты пе́рвый раз одна́ с люби́мым"	пе́рвый раз – for the first time; одна́ – alone

Лексика и грамматика

1. Свежо́ – све́жий – све́жесть *(f.)* share a common root. Find the root and write down its

meaning in English. _____. Make up two sentences with these

words. _____

_____

181

2. Запах – па́хнуть share a common root. Find the root and write down its meaning in English.

_____. Make up a sentence with "па́хнуть." Hint: remember to use

the Instrumental case with this verb._____

_____

3. Косну́ться – прикоснове́нье share a common root. Find the root and write down its meaning

in English. _____. Make up a sentence with either of these words.

_____

4. Смех – рассмея́ться – насме́шка share a common root. Find the root and write down its

meaning in English. _____. Make up two sentences with these words.

_____

_____

Вопросы для обсуждения

1. What is the atmosphere of the poem? Can you point to specific details in the text?

2. How does the man behave? What can we infer about his feelings?

3. What are the feelings of the woman?

Два́дцать пе́рвое. Ночь. Понеде́льник . . .** (1917)

Два́дцать пе́рвое. Ночь. Понеде́льник.

Очерта́нья столи́цы во мгле.   очерта́нье – outline; столи́ца – capital city; мгла – darkness

182

Сочини́л же како́й-то **безде́льник,**	сочини́ть *(Perf.)* – *here:* to invent; же – emphatic particle; безде́льник – idler
Что **быва́ет** любо́вь на **земле́.**	быва́ть *(Impf.)* – to happen; земля́ – earth
И от **ле́ности** или от **ску́ки**	ле́ность *(f.)* – laziness; ску́ка – boredom
Все **пове́рили, так** и живу́т:	пове́рить *(Perf.)* – to believe; так – *here:* like this
Ждут **свида́ний,** боя́тся **разлу́ки**	свида́ние – date; разлу́ка – separation
И любо́вные **пе́сни пою́т.**	пе́сня – song; петь *(Impf.)* – to sing
Но **ины́м открыва́ется та́йна,**	ины́е *(poet.)* – others; открыва́ться *(Impf.)* – to open, be revealed; та́йна – mystery
И **почи́ет** на них **тишина́** . . .	почива́ть *(arch.)* – to rest; тишина́ – stillness, quietude
Я на э́то **наткну́лась случа́йно**	наткну́ться *(Perf.)* – to stumble upon; случа́йно – by chance
И с тех пор **всё как бу́дто** больна́.	Всё – still; как бу́дто – as if

Лексика и грамматика

1. Очерта́нье – черта́ – черти́ть share a common root. Find the root and write down its meaning in English. _____. Make up a sentence with any of these words.

_____

2. Find the prefix and the root in "безде́льник" and write down their meanings in English._____

_____. Can you think of any other words with the same root?

_____

3. Find the prefix and the root in "свида́нье" and write down their meanings in English._____

_____. Can you think of any other words with the same root?

_____

Make up a sentence with "свида́нье." _____

4. "Как бу́дто" introduces a compararison. In the poem Akhmatova says "я как бу́дто больна́." Be a poet and make up a sentence with this expression.

_____

Вопросы для обсуждения

1. What is the poem about?

2. How does the poet characterize the person who "сочини́л, что быва́ет любо́вь на земле́"?

3. How do you understand the distinction between "все" and "ины́е" made in the poem? Where does the poet see herself?

4. Do you like the poem? Why?

Есть в бли́зости люде́й заве́тная черта́ . . .*** (1915)

This poem was dedicated to the Russian poet and literary critic Nikolai Vladimirovich Nedobrovó, who was one of Akhmatova's closest friends and who was in love with her. This poem is a reply to his poem, "С тобо́й в разлу́ке от твои́х стихо́в…" dedicated to her.

Есть в **бли́зости** люде́й **заве́тная черта́**,	бли́зость *(f.)* – closeness; заве́тная – sacred; черта́ – line
Её не **перейти́ влюблённости** и **стра́сти**, –	перейти́ *(Perf.)* – to cross; влюблённость *(f.)* – being in love; страсть *(f.)* – passion
Пусть в **жу́ткой тишине́ слива́ются уста́**,	жу́ткий – *here:* eery; тишина́ – stillness; слива́ться *(Impf.)* – to merge; уста́ *(arch.)* – lips

184

И се́рдце **рвётся** от любви́ **на ча́сти**.	рва́ться *(Impf.)* – to tear; на ча́сти *(idiom.)* – to pieces
И дру́жба здесь **бесси́льна**, и года́	бесси́льна – powerless
Высо́кого и **о́гненного** сча́стья,	высо́кий – high; о́гненный – fiery
Когда́ душа́ свобо́дна и **чужда́**	чужда́ – alien
Медли́тельной исто́ме сладостра́стья.	медли́тельный – slow; исто́ма – languor; сладостра́стье – voluptuousness
Стремя́щиеся к ней **безу́мны**, а её	стремя́щиеся – striving; безу́м/е/н – mad
Дости́гшие – поражены́ тоско́ю . . .	дости́гшие – achieved; поражены́ – stricken; тоска́ – melancholy
Тепе́рь ты по́нял, **отчего́** моё	отчего́ – why
Не **бьётся** се́рдце под твое́й руко́ю.	би́ться *(Impf.)* – to beat

Лексика и грамматика

1. Find the prefix and the root in "перейти́" and write down their meanings in English._____
_____. Can you think of any other words with the same
prefix?_____
Make up a sentence with "перейти́."_____

2. Find the prefix and the root in "бесси́льна" and write down their meanings in English._____
_____. Can you think of any other words with the same
prefix?_____

3. Find the prefix and the root in "безу́мны" and write down their meanings in English._____

_____. Can you think of any other words with the same root?

_____

Make up a sentence with "безу́мный/безу́мно."_____

_____

4. Reread the second and third stanzas. In the third stanza to what does the pronoun "к ней"

refer ? _____

5. Find all the participles in the poem (3) and write down their type and the verbs from which

they are formed._____

_____

Make up a sentence with any of these participles. _____

_____

Вопросы для обсуждения

1. What is the poem about?

2. What does the poet say about the separation that exists between lovers?

3. How do you understand the final line, "Тепе́рь ты по́нял, отчего́ моё / Не бьётся се́рдце под

твое́й руко́ю"?

Никола́й Степа́нович Гумилёв (1886–1921)

Nikolai Gumilev was one of the leading poets of the Silver Age. Along with Osip Mandelshtam and Anna Akhmatova, he belonged to the Acmeists. Acmeism was a poetic movement that emerged in Russia in 1910 under the leadership of Gumilev and Sergei Gorodetsky in response to Symbolism. The Acmeists' aesthetic ideal was a compactness of form and clarity of expression. The name of the group comes from the Greek word *acme*, meaning "the highest point." Gumilev is known also as a translator, the founder of the literary magazines *Аполло́н* (*Apollo*) and *Гиперборе́й* (*Hyperborean*), a theorist of the Acmeist movement (see his *Пи́сьма о поэ́зии*), and a literary critic. He was an intrepid traveler, and many of his poems reflect his lifelong passion for faraway lands, southern seas, and an exotic atmosphere (for example, see his poem "Жира́ф," included in this book).

Gumilev studied in the Tsarskoselsky Gymnasium, where another poet, Innokenty Annensky, was the director. Gumilev was far from a diligent student; Annensky at one point saved him from being expelled by saying, "но ведь он пи́шет стихи́" (but he writes poetry). It was at the Tsarskoselsky Gymnasium that Gumilev met Anna Akhmatova and fell in love with her.

After graduation Gumilev studied at the Sorbonne in Paris and traveled. His great interest in geography and zoology and in exotic lands led him to organize several large expeditions to Africa. From his travels Gumilev brought back many vauable artifacts that later became part of the collection of the Ethnography Museum (Kunstkamera) in St. Petersburg. In 1910 he married Anna Akhmatova, and their son Lev was born in 1912. In 1913 Gumilev organized another extensive expedition to Africa, this time to Djibouti and Somalia, jointly with the Russian Academy of Sciences. With the beginning of World War I in 1914 Gumilev volunteered for the army. For his courage during 1914–1917 he was awarded several Russian medals of distinction—the crosses of St. George. In 1918 he and Akhmatova divorced, and Gumilev married Anna Engelgard, with whom he had a daughter, but both mother and daughter died from hunger in the Leningrad blockade in 1942, twenty-one years after his death.

Gumilev continued to publish his poetry and participate in the literary life of Soviet Russia. In 1921 he was arrested on the false accusation of his having participated in a counterrevolutionary plot, and he was executed. His poetry was not published in the USSR. Gumilev was rehabilitated in 1992 after Gorbachev's policy of perestroika.

Индю́к ** (1920)

На у́тре па́мяти неве́рной,	па́мять *(f.)* – memory; неве́рный – faulty
Я вспомина́ю пёстрый луг,	вспомина́ть *(Impf.)* – to recall; пёстрый – multicolored; луг – meadow
Где ца́рствовал высокоме́рный,	ца́рствовать *(Impf.)* – to reign; высокоме́рный – haughty
Мной обожа́емый индю́к.	обожа́емый – adored; индю́к – turkey
Была́ в нём зло́ба и свобо́да,	зло́ба – spite; свобо́да – freedom
Был клюв его́ как пла́мя ал,	клюв – beak; пла́мя – flame; ал – а́лый – scarlet
И за мои́ четы́ре го́да	
Меня́ он о́стро презира́л.	о́стро – sharply; презира́ть *(Impf.)* – to despise
Ни шокола́д, ни караме́ли,	караме́ль *(f.)* – caramels
Ни анана́сная вода́	анана́сная вода́ – pineapple lemonade
Меня́ уте́шить не уме́ли	уте́шить *(Perf.)* – to comfort; уме́ть *(Impf.)* – to know how
В созна́ньи моего́ стыда́.	созна́нье – *here:* realization; стыд – shame
И вновь пришла́ беда́ больша́я,	беда́ – trouble
И стыд, и го́ре де́тских лет:	го́ре – grief
Ты, обожа́емая, зла́я,	злой – evil
Мне го́рдо отвеча́ешь: "Нет!"	го́рдо – proudly

Но всё **прохо́дит** в жи́зни **зы́бкой** —   проходи́ть *(Impf.)* – to pass; зы́бкий – shaky, unstable

Пройдёт любо́вь, пройдёт **тоска́**,   тоска́ – longing

И **вспо́мню** я тебя́ с **улы́бкой**,   вспо́мнить *(Perf.)* – to remember; улы́бка – smile

Как вспомина́ю индюка́!

Ле́ксика и грамма́тика

1. Вспо́мнить – па́мять – вспомина́ть share a common root. Find the root and write **down its**

meaning in English. _____ . Make up a sentence with **any of**

these words. _____

2. Find the prefix and the root in "проходи́ть" and write down their meanings in

English._____. Can you think of any other words with the same **root?**

_____

Make up a sentence with "проходи́ть." _____

3. Find the root in "обожа́емый" and write down its meaning in English. _____

Be a poet and make up a sentence with "обожа́ть" + *Acc.*:_____

_____

4. Find the two roots in "высокоме́рный" and write down their meanings in English._____

_____

Вопро́сы для обсужде́ния

1. What is the connection between the poet's childhood past and the present?

2. According to the poet, what characteristics do both the turkey and the heroine of the poem have in common?

3. Is it a funny poem? Why or why not? Explain.

Сон ** (1918)

This poem was dedicated to Anna Akhmatova.

Застона́л я от **сна́ дурно́го**	застона́ть – to moan; с/о/н – dream; дурно́й – bad
И **проснýлся, тя́жко скорбя́**;	проснýться *(Perf.)* – to wake up; тя́жко – deeply; скорбя́ – grieving
Сни́лось мне – ты лю́бишь **друго́го,**	сни́лось мне – I dreamed; друго́й – another
И что он **оби́дел** тебя́.	оби́деть *(Perf.)* – to hurt
Я бежа́л от мое́й **посте́ли,**	посте́ль *(f.)* – bed
Как **уби́йца** от **пла́хи** свое́й,	уби́йца – murderer; пла́ха – executioner's block
И смотре́л, как **тýскло блесте́ли**	тýскло – dimly; блесте́ть *(Impf.)* – to glimmer
Фонари́ глаза́ми **звере́й.**	фонáрь – street lamp; зверь – beast
Ах, **наве́рно** таки́м бездо́мным	наве́рно – probably
Не **блужда́л** ни оди́н челове́к	блужда́ть *(Impf.)* – to wander

В эту ночь по у́лицам тёмным,

Как по ру́слам вы́сохших рек. ру́сло – riverbed; вы́сохший – dried

Вот стою́ перед две́рью твое́ю,

Не дано́ мне ино́го пути́, No other way way is possible for me

Хоть и зна́ю, что не **посме́ю** хоть – although; посме́ть *(Perf.)* – to dare

Никогда́ в эту дверь войти́.

Он оби́дел тебя́, я зна́ю,

Хоть и бы́ло это **лишь** сном, лишь – only

Но я **всё-таки умира́ю** всё-таки – nonetheless; умира́ть *(Impf.)* – to die

Пред твои́м **закры́тым окно́м.** пред – перед – in front of; закры́тый – closed; окно́ –

window

Лексика и грамматика

1. С/о/н – сни́ться (+ *D.* subject) – со́нный – бессо́нница share a common root. Find the root and write down its meaning in English. _____. Make up two sentences with any of these words. _____

_____

Finish the following sentence: Мне сни́лось,_____

_____

2. Find the prefix and the root in "бездóмный" and write down their meanings in English.

_____. Can you think of any other words with the same

root? _____

Make up a sentence with "бездóмный."_____

3. Обúдеть – обúда – обúдно – обижáться на когó *(Acc.)* share a common root. Find the root

and write down its meaning in English. _____. Make up a

sentence with any of these words._____

_____

Вопросы для обсуждения

1. What is the atmosphere of the poem?

2. What happened in the poet's dream? How did he react?

3. How do you understand the ending: "Он обúдел тебя, я знáю, / Хоть и бы́ло это лишь
сном, / Но я всё-таки умирáю / Пред твоúм закры́тым окнóм"?

Жирáф *** (1907)

This poem was written to Anna Akhmatova.

Сегóдня, я вúжу, **осóбенно грýстен** твой взгляд	осóбенно – especially; грýст/е/н – sad; взгляд – glance
И рýки осóбенно **тóнки, колéни обня́в.**	тóнки – thin; колéни – knees; обня́в – embraced
Послýшай: далёко, далёко, на **óзере Чад**	óзеро Чад – Lake Chad in Africa

194

Изы́сканный бро́дит жира́ф.	изы́сканный – exquisite; броди́ть *(Impf.)* – to wander, жира́ф – giraffe
Ему́ **грацио́зная стро́йность** и **не́га** дана́,	грацио́зный – graceful; стро́йность *(f.)* – slenderness; не́га – bliss
И **шку́ру** его́ **украша́ет волше́бный узо́р,**	шку́ра – hide; украша́ть *(Impf.)* – to decorate; волше́бный – magical; узо́р – design
С кото́рым **равня́ться осме́лится** то́лько луна́,	равня́ться *(Impf.)* – to equal; осме́литься *(Perf.)* – to dare
Дробя́сь и **кача́ясь** на **вла́ге** широ́ких озёр.	дробя́сь – splitting; кача́ясь – rocking; вла́га – moisture
Вдали́ он **подо́бен цветны́м паруса́м корабля́,**	вдали́ – at a distance; подо́бен – similar; цветно́й – colored; па́рус – sail; кора́бль – ship
И **бег** его́ **пла́вен,** как **ра́достный пти́чий полёт.**	бег – gait; пла́в/е/н – smooth; ра́достный – joyful; пти́чий – bird's; полёт – flight
Я зна́ю, что мно́го **чуде́сного** ви́дит земля́,	чуде́сный – wonderful
Когда́ на **зака́те** он **пря́чется** в **мра́морный грот.**	зака́т – sunset; пря́таться *(Impf.)* – to hide, мра́морный – marble; грот – grotto
Я зна́ю весёлые **ска́зки таи́нственных стран**	ска́зка – fairy tale; таи́нственный – mysterious; страна́ – country

Про чёрную дéву, про **страсть** молодóго **вождя́,** дéва – maiden; страсть *(f.)* – passion; вождь – leader

Но ты **сли́шком** дóлго **вдыха́ла тяжёлый тума́н,** сли́шком – too; вдыха́ть *(Impf.)* – to inhale; тяжёлый – heavy; тума́н – mist

Ты вéрить не хóчешь во чтó-нибудь **крóме дождя́.** крóме (+ *Gen.*) – except; дождь – rain

И как я тебé расскажу́ **про тропи́ческий** сад, про (+ *Acc.*) – about; тропи́ческий – tropical

Про **стрóйные** пáльмы, про **зáпах немы́слимых трав.** стрóйный – slender; зáпах – scent; немы́слимый – inconceivable; трава́ – *here:* herb

Ты **плáчешь?** Послу́шай . . . далёко, на óзере Чад плáкать *(Impf.)* – to cry

Изы́сканный брóдит жира́ф.

Лексика и грамматика

1. Вдали́ – далёко – далёкий share a common root. Find the root and write down its meaning in English. _____. Make up two sentences with these words.

_____

_____

2. Find the prefix and the root in "украша́ть" and write down their meanings in English. _____. Can you think of any other words with the same root?

_____

Make up a sentence with "украша́ть."_____

3. Find the root in "ра́достный" and write down its meaning in English._____

_____. Can you think of any other words with the same root?

_____

Make up a sentence with "ра́достный."_____

4. Find the prefix and the root in "осме́литься" and write down their meanings in English.

_____. List other words with the same root._____

_____

Make up a sentence with "осме́литься." _____

_____

5. Find the the root in "равня́ться" and write down its meaning in English._____

_____. Can you think of any other words with the same root?

_____

Make up a sentence with any of these words._____

_____

6. Reread the third stanza. Can you find two nouns describing the giraffe that are formed from

verbs of motion? _____

7. Reread the fourth stanza. The preposition "кро́ме + Gen." means "except." Be a poet and

make up a sentence with this preposition. _____

1. What is the atmosphere of the poem?

2. Where are the woman who is being addressed and the poet?

3. Why does he want to talk to her about "Весёлые ска́зки таи́нственных стран"?

4. How are the two worlds of reality and fairy tales contrasted? Can you point to specific examples in the poem?

О тебе́ *** (1918)

О тебе́, о тебе́, о тебе́,

Ничего́, ничего́ обо мне́!

В **челове́ческой, тёмной судьбе́**	челове́ческий – human; тёмный – dark; судьба́ – fate
Ты – **крыла́тый призы́в** к **вышине́.**	крыла́тый – winged; призы́в – call; вышина́ – height
Благоро́дное се́рдце твоё –	благоро́дный – noble; се́рдце – heart
Сло́вно герб отоше́дших времён.	сло́вно – like; герб – coat of arms; отоше́дший – passed, gone by; времена́ – times
Освяща́ется им **бытиё**	освяща́ться *(Impf.)* – to sanctify; бытиё – existence
Всех **земны́х,** всех бескры́лых **племён.**	земно́й – earthly; пле́мя – tribe
Если **звёзды, ясны́** и **горды́,**	звезда́ – star; я́с/е/н – clear; горд – proud
Отверну́тся от на́шей земли́,	отверну́ться *(Perf.)* – to turn away
У неё есть две лу́чших звезды́:	
Это – **сме́лые о́чи** твои.	сме́лый – brave; о́чи *(arch.)* – eyes

И когда́ **золото́й серафи́м**	золото́й – golden; серафи́м – seraph
Протруби́т, что **испо́лнился срок**,	протруби́ть (Perf.) – to blow the trumpet; испо́лниться *(Perf.) – here:* to come; срок – *here:* time
Мы **подни́мем** тогда́ перед ним,	подня́ть *(Perf.)* – to raise
Как **защи́ту**, твой бе́лый **плато́к**.	защи́та – defense; плат/о́/к – scarf
Звук замрёт в **задрожа́вшей трубе́,**	звук – sound; замере́ть *(Perf.)* – to die away; задрожа́вший – trembling; труба́ – trumpet
Серафи́м **пропадёт** в вышине́ . . .	пропа́сть *(Perf.)* – to disappear
. . . О тебе́, о тебе́, о тебе́,	
Ничего́, ничего́ обо мне́!	

Лексика и грамматика

1. Земля́ – земно́й – неземно́й share a common root. Find the root and write down its meaning in English. _____. Make up a sentence with any of these words.

_____

2. Find the prefix and the root in "бескры́лый" and write down their meanings in English._____ _____. Do you know any other words with the same root? _____

3. Find the two roots in "благоро́дный" and write down their meanings in English._____

199

_____. Can you guess what "благоразу́мный" means?

_____

Make up two sentences with "благоро́дный." _____

_____

4. What aspect is used more frequently in the poem? What is the reason for this aspectual

choice?_____

5. Indicate all the uses of the Prepositional case, not counting the repetitions

(5)._____

Вопросы для обсуждения

1. What is the poem about?

2. How does the poet see the woman he addresses? Can you point to specific examples in the poem?

3. What can be inferred about his feelings?

4. What is the role of "золото́й серафи́м" in the poem?

Влади́мир Влади́мирович Маяко́вский (1893–1930)

Vladimir Mayakovsky is considered to be one of the foremost representatives of Russian

Futurism. He is known as a poet, playwright, and poster artist. He also worked in film as an actor,

screenwriter, and director, and he directed his own plays.

Mayakovsky was born in Georgia into the family of a forest ranger, but after the sudden death of

his father in 1906, his family moved to Moscow. Very early in his life Mayakovsky became

interested in Marxism and joined the Russian Social Democratic Party, where he would later

become a member of the Bolshevik faction. He joined the Moscow Art School in 1911 but was

expelled in 1914 for his political activities. He was arrested several times and spent some time in

prison. At that time he became friends with another prominent Futurist poet, David Burlyuk, and

the two began a collaboration and published the Futurist manifesto *A Slap in the Face of Public

Taste (Пощёчина обще́ственному вку́су);* it contained Mayakovsky's first poems.

The novelty of Mayakovsky's poetry was evident from the very beginning, not only in its poetic language but even in the way his poems were typeset because new printing techniques were used to set the text—for example, the short column *(стóлбик)* and the staircase *(лéсенка),* which reflects the placement of pauses and allows for greater expressiveness.

Mayakovsky volunteered for World War I but was rejected for "political unrealiability," so he worked as a draftsman. His first long narrative poem, "A Cloud in Trousers" (Óблако в штанáх), published in 1915, was about love, revolution, art, and religion from the point of view of an unhappy lover and poet. Mayakovsky himself described the meaning of his poem, which contained four parts, as "Down with love, down with art, down with the social order, down with religion!," calling for the destruction of bourgeois values and conventions. In that same year he met Lilya Brik, the wife of his publisher, Osip Brik, and she became Mayakovsky's muse.

Mayakovsky was an enthusiastic supporter of the October Revolution of 1917, and he began to work in the Russian State Telegraph Agency (ROSTA), creating satirical posters with graphics and text known as "Okna ROSTA." Over three years he created 1,100 posters. In 1919 he published a collection of his works from 1909 to 1919, *Всё сочинённое Владúмиром Маякóвским,* and his polularity grew rapidly. He gave many public readings and lectures in the Soviet Union and abroad, including a lecture tour in the United States in 1925. He wrote many poems about his travels and an essay, "Моё открыʹтие Амéрики" (My Discovery of America).

Mayakovsky was an active spokesman for the new regime and even created a group, ComFut—Communistic Futurism (Коммунисти́ческий Футури́зм). In 1922–1928 he was an active member of the Left Art Front (LEF) and edited the magazine *LEF*. Later he left the LEF and founded the Revolutionary Art Front (REF).

In 1930 Mayakovsky had a series of disappointments in his personal and professional life. For one thing, his play *The Bathhouse ("Ба́ня")* was seen as a huge failure; for another, his French love, Tatyana Yakovleva, to whom he wrote two celebrated love poems ("Письмо́ Татья́не Яковлевой" and "Письмо́ това́рищу Костро́ву о су́щности любви́") and to whom he even proposed, did not accept him and married someone else. During the last year of his life he met and fell in love with a young actress, Veronika Polonskaya, but she was married and was not prepared to leave her husband. Mayakovsky, who was prone to bouts of depression and who had (according to Lilya Brik) twice tried to shoot himself before, wrote his last poem, "Любо́вная ло́дка разби́лась о быт" (The loveboat has crashed on the humdrum of everyday life) on April 12, and on April 14, 1930, he shot himself in his Moscow apartment in front of Veronika Polonskaya while the Briks were in Paris. In his will he left all of his poetic legacy to the Briks and named Lilya as a family member.

Проща́ние * (1925)

В авто́,

авто́ – automobile

после́дний франк разменя́в.

после́дний – last; франк – franc; разменя́ть *(Perf.) – here:* to

	break (a coin)
– В котóром часý на **Марсéль**? –	Марсель – Marseille
Парúж	
бежúт,	
провожáя меня,	провожáть *(Impf.)* – to see off
во всей	
невозмóжной красé.	невозмóжный – impossible; красá – beauty
Подступáй	подступáть (к + *D.; Impf.)* – to come up
к глазáм,	
разлýки жúжа,	разлýка – parting; жúжа – moisture
сéрдце	сéрдце – heart
мне	
сантиментáльностью расквáсь!	сантиментáльность *(f.)* – sentimentality; расквáсить *(Perf., colloq.)* – to make slushy
Я хотéл бы	
жить	
и умерéть в Парúже,	
éсли б нé было	If a land like this had not existed
такóй землú –	
Москвá.	

Лексика и грамматика

1. Find the prefix and the root in "разменя́ть" and write down their meanings in English.

_____. Can you think of any other words with the same root?

_____

Make up a sentence with "разменя́ть."_____

2. Find the prefix and the root in "провожа́ть" and write down their meanings in English.

_____. Make up a sentence with "провожа́ть."_____

_____

3. Краса́ – прекра́сный – укра́сить share a common root. Find the root and write down its

meaning in English. _____ . Make up two sentences with any of

these words._____

_____

4. Find the prefix and the root in "невозмо́жный" and write down their meanings in English.

_____. Can you think of any other words with the same

root? _____

Make up a sentence with "невозмо́жно." Remember that in English the subject needs to be in

the Dative: Мне/Ему/Ей/Нам невозмо́жно. . . . _____

_____

5. Подступа́ть (к чему; *D.*) – ступи́ть (во что; *Acc.*) – вступле́ние share a common root. Find

the root and write down its meaning in English. _____. Make up a

sentence with any of these words._____

_____

6. Be a poet and finish the following sentence: Я б хотéл/а_____

_____

Вопросы для обсуждения

1. What is the poem about?

2. What are the poet's feelings toward Paris?

3. How do conversational and formal registers of speech collide in the poem? Cite specific examples.

4. What city is the poet's favorite? Why does he refer to Moscow as земля?

А вы моглú бы? *** (1913)

This seemingly obscure Futuristic poem was written after a meal at a restaurant where Mayakovsky had studied the menu the day before. This poem is very rich in imagery that grows out of everyday items as seen by a Futurist (for example, red wine becomes paint in a glass, the tin mold of a fish aspic turns into a fish, the imprints of fish scales on the aspic become the slanted cheekbones of the ocean, etc.).

Я срáзу смáзал **кáрту бýдня,**	смáзать *(Perf.)* – to smear; кáрта бýдня (from *Fr. carte du jour*) – *here:* menu of the day
плеснýвши крáску из стакáна;	плеснýвши крáску – having spilled the paint
я показáл на **блюде стýдня**	блюдо – platter; стýд/е/нь – fish in aspic
косьíе скýлы океáна.	косóй – slanting; скýлы – cheekbones; океáн – ocean
На **чешуé жестя́ной ры́бы**	чешуя́ *(sg.)* – scales; жестя́ный – tin (describing the tin fish mold)

прочёл я зо́вы но́вых губ.   прочёл *(Perf., conv.)* – read; зо́в – call; гу́бы – lips

А вы

ноктю́рн сыгра́ть   ноктю́рн – nocturne

могли́ бы

на **фле́йте водосто́чных труб?**   фле́йта – flute; водосто́чная труба́ – gutter

Лексика и грамматика

1. Identify all the Perfective verbs in the poem (4) and list them here, indicating their

Imperfective counterparts and their meanings in English. _____

_____

_____

Make up sentences with сыгра́ть and показа́ть (кому) _____

_____

2. Звать – зов – называ́ть – назва́ние share a common root. Find the root and write down its

meaning in English. _____. Make up two sentences with any of

these words._____

_____

3. Find the two roots in "водосто́чный" and write down their meanings in English._____

_____

Make up a sentence with the verb течь *(Impf.)* (to flow). "Течь" is conjugated exactly like the verb "печь" (to bake). (я теку́, ты течёшь, он/а течёт, мы течём, вы течёте, они теку́т.)

_____

4. Be a poet and finish the following conditional sentence: А вы могли бы_____

_____?

Вопросы для обсуждения

1. How does the poet describe the everyday world?

2. In your opinion, what makes this poem Futuristic? Give specific examples.

3. How do you understand the last sentence?

4. Do you like the poem? Why or why not?

Послу́шайте! *** (1914)

Послу́шайте!

Ведь, е́сли звёзды **зажига́ют**	зажига́ть *(Impf.)* – to light up
зна́чит – это кому́-нибу́дь ну́жно?	зна́чить – to mean
Зна́чит – кто-то хо́чет, чтобы они́ бы́ли?	
Зна́чит – кто-то называ́ет эти **плево́чки**	плево́ч/е/к *(dim.)* – плев/о/к – spit
жемчу́жиной?	жемчу́жина – pearl
И, **надрыва́ясь**	надрыва́ясь – straining oneself
в **мете́лях полу́денной пы́ли,**	мете́ль *(f.)* – blizzard; полу́денный – midday; пыль *(f.)* – dust

врыва́ется к Бо́гу,	врыва́ться (куда, к кому; *Impf.*) – to burst in on, rush toward
бои́тся, что **опозда́л**,	боя́ться *(Impf.)* – to be afraid; опозда́ть *(Perf.)* – to be late
пла́чет,	пла́кать *(Impf.)* – to cry
целу́ет ему **жи́листую** ру́ку,	целова́ть *(Impf.)* – to kiss; жи́листый – veiny
про́сит –	
чтоб обяза́тельно была́ звезда́! –	
клянётся –	кля́сться *(Impf.)* – to swear
не **перенесёт** эту беззвёздную **му́ку**!	перенести́ *(Perf.)* – to endure; му́ка – torture
А по́сле	
хо́дит **трево́жный**,	трево́жный – worried
но споко́йный **нару́жно**.	нару́жно – outwardly
Говори́т кому́-то:	
"**Ведь тепе́рь тебе́ ничего́**?	Now you are doing OK?
Не стра́шно?	
Да?!"	
Послу́шайте!	
Ведь, е́сли звёзды	
зажига́ют –	
зна́чит – э́то кому́-нибудь ну́жно?	
Зна́чит – э́то **необходи́мо**,	необходи́мо – necessary
чтобы ка́ждый ве́чер	

над **кры́шами**   кры́ша – roof

загора́лась **хоть** одна́ звезда́?!   хоть – *here:* at least

Лексика и грамматика

1. Find the prefixes and the root in "необходи́мо" and write down their meanings in English.

_____. Can you think of any other words with the same root?

_____

Make up a sentence with "необходи́мо." Remember that the subject will be in the Dative

(Ему/ей/мне/вам необходи́мо. . . .) _____

2. Find the prefix and the root in "беззвёздный" and write down their meanings in English.

_____. Can you think of any other words with the same prefix?

_____

Make up a sentence with "беззвёздный."_____

3. Find the prefix and the root in "перенести́" and write down their meanings in English.

_____. Can you think of any other words with the same

root? _____

Make up a sentence with "перенести́." _____

4. Reread the poem and list all the Imperfective verbs (11)._____

_____

Why is the Imperfective aspect used throught the poem?_____

_____

Вопросы для обсуждения

1. What does the poet want to assert?

2. What does the poet ask of God?

3. Why does the poet want to have at least one star lit in the sky? How do you understand this last sentence?

Серге́й Алекса́ндрович Есе́нин (1895–1925)

Sergey Yesenin remains one of the most beloved and popular lyric poets of the twentieth century in Russia. He was born to a peasant family in the village of Konstantinovo near the city of Ryazan, located 122 miles southeast of Moscow. He started writing poems when he was nine years old, and at seventeen he moved to Moscow to study at the university. In 1915 he came to St. Petersburg and quickly became known in literary circles. He met his literary idol, Alexander Blok, who liked his poetry and introduced him to many literary figures of the time, such as the poets Sergey Gorodetsky, Nikolai Kluev, and Andrey Bely.

Yesenin first gained public recognition as a "peasant poet," ("крестья́нский поэт") alongside his older friend Nikolai Kluev, another "peasant poet." Both were interested in Russian folklore and the oral tradition, and they wanted to incorporate folk motifs and language in their poetry. Sometimes Yesenin and Kluev even recited their poetry dressed in peasant folk costumes.

In 1918 Yesenin, with the poets Anatoly Merinhof and Vadim Shershenevich, formed the new literary movement of Imaginists. The Imaginists wanted to distance themselves from the Futurists, and they created a poetry using a lot of metaphors and sequences of arresting and uncommon images. They published a literary magazine called *Гостúница для путешéствующих в прекрáсном* (*Guesthouse for Travelers in the Beautiful*). That was a very fruitful and exciting period for Russian poetry and innovations in literary form since many great poets of the Silver Age were working at that time. The group broke up in 1925, but its influence was felt for many years afterward.

In 1922 Yesenin married the celebrated American dancer Isadora Duncan, whom he had met at one of her performances in Russia, and he accompanied her on tour to Europe and the United States. Isadora did not know Russian, and Yesenin spoke almost no English. Their marriage did not last, and he returned to Russia in 1923. In the last period of his life Yesenin suffered from alcoholism and had a mental breakdown. Two days after his release from the hospital where he was being treated for depression, he slashed his wrists, wrote his last poem in his own blood, and hanged himself in the Hotel Angleterre in St. Petersburg.

До свида́нья, друг мой, до свида́нья . . . * (1925)

This is the last poem that Yesenin wrote before he committed suicide on December 28, 1925.

До свида́нья, дру́г мой, до свида́нья.

Ми́лый мой, ты **у меня́ в груди́**. грудь *(f.)* – chest; *here:* you are in my heart

Предназна́ченное расста́ванье предназна́ченное – predestined; расста́ванье – parting

Обеща́ет встре́чу впереди́. обеща́ть – to promise; встре́ча – meeting; впереди́ – ahead

До свида́нья, друг мой, **без руки́**, без **сло́ва,** без – without; рука – hand; сло́во – word

Не грусти́ и не печа́ль бровей́, – грусти́ть – to be sad; печа́лить – *here:* to

cast down, lower; бровь *(f.)* – eyebrow

В э́той жи́зни **умира́ть** не **но́во,** умира́ть – to die; но́во – *(cf.* но́вый*)* – new

Но и жить, **коне́чно,** не **нове́й.** коне́чно – certainly; нове́й *(comp.)* – newer

Лексика и грамматика

1. The preposition "без" means "without" and is followed by the Genitive case. Make up a

sentence with this contruction._____

_____

2. Find the imperatives in the poem (2) and list them here. _____

3. "Новée" is the comparative form of "но́вый." Make up a sentence with this word. Remember

to use the Genitive case after the compartive form._____

216

4. "Обеща́ть/пообеща́ть кому" means "to promise someone" and is used with the Dative case.

What does "обеща́ние" mean?_____. Make up a sentence with

this verb._____

5. "Коне́чно" means "certainly, surely." Make up a sentence with this word._____

Вопросы для обсуждения

1. Whom do you think the poet is addressing?

2. How do you understand "без руки́, без сло́ва"?

3. How do you understand the lines "Предназна́ченное расста́ванье / Обеща́ет встре́чу впереди́?" Where do you think that meeting would take place?

4. Reread the last two lines of the poem: "В э́той жи́зни умира́ть не но́во, / Но и жить, коне́чно, не нове́й." What can we say about the poet's beliefs? How does this poem compare to Lermontov's "И ску́чно, и гру́стно . . ." and to Blok's "Ночь, у́лица, фона́рь, апте́ка"?

5. Do you agree or disagree with these views? Explain your point of view.

Отговори́ла ро́ща золота́я . . . ** (1924)

Отговори́ла ро́ща золота́я	отговори́ть *(Perf.)* – to finish talking; ро́ща – grove
Берёзовым, весёлым языко́м,	берёзовый *(adj.; cf.* берёза*)* – birch
И **журавли́**, печа́льно **пролета́я**,	жура́вль – crane; пролета́я – flying by
Уж не **жале́ют** бо́льше ни о ко́м.	уж – уже́ – *here:* no longer; жале́ть кого *or* о ком
	– to have pity on someone

217

Кого́ жале́ть? **Ведь** ка́ждый в **ми́ре стра́нник**	ведь – *(emphatic)* – *here:* after all; мир – world; стра́нник – pilgrim
Пройдёт, зайдёт и **вновь оста́вит** дом.	вновь – again; оста́вить *(Perf.)* – to leave, abandon
О всех **уше́дших гре́зит конопля́ник**	уше́дшие – departed; гре́зить *(poet.)* – to dream; конопля́ник – hemp field
С **широ́ким ме́сяцем** над голубы́м **прудо́м**.	широ́кий – wide; ме́сяц – crescent; пруд – pond
Стою́ оди́н **среди́ равни́ны го́лой**,	среди́ – *here:* in the middle; равни́на – plain; го́лый – naked
А журавле́й **отно́сит ве́тер в даль**,	относи́ть *(Impf.)* – to carry away; ве́т/е/р – wind; даль *(f., poet)* – distance
Я **по́лон дум о ю́ности** весёлой,	по́лон – full of; ду́ма *(poet.)* – thought; ю́ность *(f.)* – youth
Но ничего́ в **проше́дшем** мне не жаль.	проше́дшее – past; жаль (кому; English subject is in *D.*) – to regret
Не **жаль мне лет, растра́ченных напра́сно**,	лет *(Gen. pl.)* – years; растра́ченный – spent; напра́сно – in vain
Не жаль души́ **сире́невую цветь**.	сире́невый *(f.; cf.* сирень) – lilac; цветь *(f., auth.)* – bloom
В саду́ **гори́т костёр ряби́ны** кра́сной,	гори́т – to burn; костёр – fire; ряби́на – ash berry
Но никого́ не мо́жет он **согре́ть**.	согре́ть *(Perf.)* – to warm up

Не **обгоря́т ряби́новые ки́сти**,

обгоре́ть *(Perf.)* – to get burned; ряби́новый *(adj.)* – ash berry; кисть *(f.)* – *here:* bunch

От **желтизны́** не **пропадёт трава́**.

желтизна́ – *cf.* жёлтый; пропа́сть *(Perf.)* – to disappear; трава́ – grass

Как де́рево **роня́ет ти́хо ли́стья**,

де́рево – tree; роня́ть – to drop; ти́хо – quietly; ли́стья – leaves

Так я роня́ю гру́стные слова́.

И если вре́мя, ве́тром **размета́я**,

размета́я – sweeping

Сгребёт их все в оди́н **нену́жный ком**.

сгрести́ *(Perf.)* – to rake up; нену́жный – unwanted, useless; ком – ball

Скажи́те так . . . что ро́ща золота́я

Отговори́ла **ми́лым** языко́м.

ми́лый – sweet

Лексика и грамматика

1. Find the prefix and the root in "отговори́ть" and write down their meanings in English.

_____

Give an example of another verb with the same prefix._____

2. Find the prefix and the root in "пролета́я" and write down their meanings in

English._____

Give an example of another verb with the same root. _____

3. Find the prefixes in "пройдёт" and "зайдёт"; write down their meanings and the meanings of

the verbs in English. _____

Make up sentences with "пройти" and "зайти." _____

_____

4. "Среди" + чего *(Gen.)*. Make up a sentence with this preposition. _____

_____

5. Find all the gerunds (2) _____

and participles (3) in the poem. _____

6. Reread the line "Не жаль мне лет, растраченных напрасно." "Жаль" is the poetic form of

"жалко." The subject used with this expression is in the Dative case and the object is in the

Genitive. Be a poet and finish the following sentence: Не жаль мне _____

_____

Вопросы для обсуждения

1. What is the season described in the poem?

2. What imagery associated with fall is mentioned in the poem? Point to specific examples in the text.

3. How do you understand the lines "В саду горит костёр рябины красной, / Но никого не может он согреть"?

4. Compare this poem to Pushkin's "Осень (отрывок)" above. How does the mood differ in Yesenin's poem?

5. What connection does the poet make between the season and one's emotional state?

6. What are some of the themes mentioned in the poem?

Не жале́ю, не зову́, не пла́чу . . . ***(1921)

Sophia Tolstaya, the granddaughter of Lev Tolstoy and Yesenin's last wife, recalled in her memoirs that Yesenin said that this poem was written under the influence of one of Gogol's lyrical digressions in his novel *Dead Souls*. The passage to which Yesenin alludes is in the opening of Gogol's chapter six, which concludes with the following lines: "что пробуди́ло бы в пре́жние го́ды живо́е движе́нье в лице́, смех и немо́лчные ре́чи, то скользи́т тепе́рь ми́мо, и безуча́стное молча́ние храня́т мои недви́жные уста́. О моя ю́ность! о моя све́жесть!" (What would in previous years have aroused lively movement in the face, laughter, and incessant speeches slips past me now, and indifferent silence seals my motionless lips. Oh my youth! Oh, my freshness!)

Не **жале́ю**, не **зову́**, не **пла́чу**,	жале́ть – to regret; звать – to call; пла́кать – to cry
Всё пройдёт, как с бе́лых **я́блонь дым**.	я́блоня – apple tree; дым – smoke
Увяда́нья зо́лотом охва́ченный,	увяда́нье *(poet.)* –fading; зо́лото – gold; охва́ченный – *here:* overtaken
Я не бу́ду бо́льше молоды́м.	
Ты тепе́рь не так уж бу́дешь би́ться,	Now you will no longer beat this way
Се́рдце, тро́нутое холодко́м,	се́рдце – heart; тро́нутый – touched; холод/о/к – cold
И **страна́ берёзового си́тца**	страна́ – country; берёзовый – birch; сит/е/ц – calico
Не **зама́нит шля́ться босико́м**.	замани́ть *(Perf.)* – to lure; шля́ться *(colloq.)* – hang about; босико́м – barefoot
Дух бродя́жий, ты всё **ре́же**, ре́же	дух – spirit, бродя́жий – vagabond; ре́же *(comp.)* ре́дкий – seldom
Расшеве́ливаешь пла́мень уст.	расшеве́ливать – to stir; пла́мень – flame; уста́ *(arch.)* – lips

О моя **утра́ченная све́жесть**,	утра́ченный *(poet.)* – lost; све́жесть *(f.)* – freshness
Бу́йство глаз и **полово́дье чувств**.	бу́йство – *here:* mischief; полово́дье – flood; чу́вство – feeling
Я тепе́рь **скупе́е** стал в **жела́ньях**,	скупе́е *(comp.; cf.* скупо́й*)* – stingy, sparing; жела́нье – desire
Жизнь моя, **иль ты присни́лась мне?**	иль ты присни́лась мне? – or did I see you in a dream?
Сло́вно я весе́нней **гу́лкой ра́нью**	сло́вно – as if; гу́лкий – resonant; рань *(f., colloq.)* – early morning hour
Проскака́л на ро́зовом коне́.	проскака́ть *(Perf.)* – to gallop by; ро́зовый – rose-colored; конь – horse
Все́ мы, все́ мы в э́том ми́ре **тле́нны**,	тле́нный *(poet.)* – *here:* temporal, of the earth
Ти́хо льётся с клёнов ли́стьев медь . . .	ти́хо – quietly; ли́ться – to pour; клён – maple; лист – leaf; медь *(f.)* – copper
Будь же ты **вове́к благослове́нно**,	вове́к – forever; благослове́нно – blessed
Что пришло́ **процве́сть** и умере́ть.	процве́сть *(aut.)* – to bloom

Лексика и грамматика

1. Write down all the verbs in the poem and analyze the aspectual choices._____

_____

Which aspect predominates and why? _____

2. Find the prefix and the root in "пройдёт" and write down their meanings in English._____

_____. Make up a sentence with "пройдёт." _____

_____

3. Find the prefix and the root in "процвести" and write down their meanings in English. _____

_____. Can you think of any other words with the same root?

_____

4. Make up a sentence with "заманить кого куда" (to lure someone somewhere). _____

_____

5. Be a poet and finish the following sentence: Мне приснилось, что_____

_____

Вопросы для обсуждения

1. What is the theme of the poem?

2. What is the author lamenting?

3. How is the metaphor of fall used in the poem? What are the metaphors related to the passing of time? Find specific examples in the text.

4. How do you understand the lines "Словно я весенней гулкой ранью / Проскакал на розовом коне"? Why is that image used in the poem?

5. What is the mood in the finale? What does the poet find "благословенно"? Why does the poem end this way?